D0358204

Honours and Titles

London: H M S O

HMSO publications are available from:

HMSO Publications Centre
(Mail, fax and telephone orders only)
PO Box 276, London SW8 5DT
Telephone orders 0171 873 9090
General enquiries 0171 873 0011
(queuing system in operation for both numbers)
Fax orders 0171 873 8200

HMSO Bookshops
49 High Holborn, London WC1V 6HB
(counter service only)
0171 873 0011 Fax 0171 831 1326
68-69 Bull Street, Birmingham B4 6AD
0121 236 9696 Fax 0121 236 9699
33 Wine Street, Bristol BS1 2BQ
0117 9264306 Fax 0117 9294515
9-21 Princess Street, Manchester M60 8AS
0161 834 7201 Fax 0161 833 0634
16 Arthur Street, Belfast BT1 4GD
01232 238451 Fax 01232 235401
71 Lothian Road, Edinburgh EH3 9AZ
0131 479 3141 Fax 0131 479 3142
The HMSO Oriel Bookshop
The Friary, Cardiff CF1 4AA
01222 395548 Fax 01222 384347

HMSO's Accredited Agents
(see Yellow Pages)

and through good booksellers

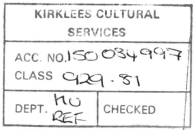

Contents

Acknowledgments

We wish to record our thanks to those kind people who have read the draft and made invaluable suggestions: The Lord Lyon King of Arms; Garter Principal King of Arms; Ceremonial Branch, Cabinet Office; Central Chancery of the Orders of Knighthood; Lord Chancellor's Department, House of Lords; Constitutional Unit, Home Office; the Registrar, Royal Archives, Windsor Castle; Press Office, Buckingham Palace; Lord Advocate's Department; The Scottish Office, Home Department.

Two fundamental works: Helen Miller, *Henry VIII and the English Peerage* and David Starkey and others, *The English Court: from the Wars of the Roses to the Civil War* have assisted us on the complexities of peerage history and the development of the royal household.

We would also like to thank Mr Russell Malloch for his helpful suggestions, especially with regard to decorations and medals.

Introduction

Within the framework of a democratic form of government Britain[1] has retained its monarchy, its peerage and its Orders of Knighthood and Chivalry. All derive their origins from past centuries. Queen Elizabeth II traces her descent from Egbert, king of Wessex, who united all England under his sovereignty in 829. There has been only one break in the English monarchy's continuity during the 11 centuries of its existence. This was the Commonwealth declared in May 1649 and ruled by the Lords Protector Oliver Cromwell (1653–58) and Richard Cromwell (1658–59). Thus the monarchy existed four centuries before Parliament and three centuries before the law courts. The peerage and Orders of Knighthood have been modified and adapted to meet changed circumstances. A factor which may have helped has been the extent of social mobility. Not every descendant of a sovereign or a peer necessarily inherits royal or noble rank. New peerages have been, and are, regularly conferred on commoners.

This book describes which people in Britain are royal. It also describes the categories and degrees of nobility, the precedence and titles of peers and of dignitaries of the established Churches, and the privileges and obligations associated with the peerage. It also gives the titles, honours and distinctions which may be borne by citizens, and the system of initials or forms of

---

[1] The term 'Britain' is used informally in this book to mean the United Kingdom of Great Britain and Northern Ireland. 'Great Britain' comprises England, Scotland and Wales.

address by which these are indicated. It describes how recipients of honours are chosen and how honours are bestowed, and takes account of the changes to the honours system which the Government introduced in 1993. It includes the honours and titles derived from the Sovereign, who is the 'fount of all honour'. It also includes certain other marks of distinction or status (whether awarded by a certain institution or bestowed by custom) which are commonly in use.

Throughout, the historical background to the development of particular aspects of honours and titles is described. The date in brackets given after a peerage is the date of creation—thus '(cr.1694)'.

The system of titles is complex, and the historical evolution of some peerages extremely so, which can cause difficulties for, and give rise to solecisms by, people both from overseas and from Britain itself. Examples abound. Thus a respectable London broadsheet in 1995 can refer to the King of Norway as 'His Royal Highness' or to a senior government minister as 'Baroness Lynda Chalker', or to a peeress from Hong Kong as 'Baroness Lydia Dunn'. A strange departure was a tabloid reference to the Dowager Duchess of Northumberland as 'Duchess Elizabeth Percy'. Another tabloid reference had the Hon. Nicholas Soames, a Minister of State, as Lord Nicholas Soames. The Deputy Chairman of the Association of District Councils of England and Wales and the Chairman of the Consumer Council have been regularly, and wrongly, referred to as 'Lady Elizabeth Anson' and 'Lady Judith Wilcox'. Even lists of government press notices can refer to another senior government minister as 'Lord Douglas-Hamilton'. Nor has it been correct to call the Princess of Wales 'Princess Diana'. This book aims to explain the basics of the system as clearly as possible and to help those who find the subject confusing. Those who wish to pursue a subject more closely are referred to Further Reading on p. 146.

For illustrative purposes, some fictitious titles have been used: the dukedoms of Bonchester and Drumour (the former with the family name Ormont), the marquessate of Fulbeck (family name Smythe), the earldom of Framville (including the viscountcy of FitzHenry, which is also the family name), the viscountcy of Liverton (family name Butler) and the barony of Blencarn.

The Royal Family

Only the Sovereign and certain members of the Sovereign's family are royal. It is possible, as will be seen, for near descendants of the Sovereign to be commoners.

The Sovereign

The reigning monarch is Her Majesty The Queen (or His Majesty The King). The full title of the present Queen in Britain, used only on the most formal occasions, is 'Elizabeth the Second by the Grace of God of the United Kingdom of Great Britain and Northern Ireland and of Her other Realms and Territories Queen, Head of the Commonwealth, Defender of the Faith'. The coinage bears the abbreviated Latin inscription 'Elizabeth II D.G. Reg. F.D.' (or 'Fid. Def.'), short for the Latin 'Dei Gratia Regina Fidei Defensor' (By the Grace of God Queen, Defender of the Faith—see p. 7).

The form of the royal title varies in the other Commonwealth countries of which the Queen is head of State. All these forms include, however, the phrase 'Head of the Commonwealth'.

The Queen is in Britain the 'fount of all honour' for the bestowal of all new dignities, including peerages, membership of the orders of knighthood and chivalry, and national medals and decorations.

The Royal Line and Styles

The present Queen is the 41st Sovereign of England since the Norman Conquest and the accession of the Duke of Normandy, as King William I of England, in 1066. There have been various changes of dynasty since then, but all new dynasties have been related to the previous one.

William I and his successors claimed feudal overlordship over Welsh princes and the Kings of Scots. They also came to possess considerable lands in France. Wales was brought under English rule at the end of the 13th century. English rule over all Ireland, begun in the 12th century, was gradually established under the Tudor dynasty (1485–1603). In 1603 King James VI of Scots succeeded to the English throne and united the crowns of Scotland and England. In 1707, under Queen Anne, England and Scotland were formally united. King George I, first king of the Hanoverian dynasty, in default of Stuart Protestant heirs, was called to the throne after the death of Queen Anne.

William I was styled 'King of the English' and 'Duke of Normandy'. King Henry II (1154–89), the first Plantagenet, was 'King of England, Duke of Normandy and Aquitaine, and Count of Anjou'.[2] He later added 'Lord of Ireland'. Normandy was lost to the English Crown in 1204, during King John's war with Philip II of France, a fact recognised in 1259. Thereafter the King no longer called himself 'Duke of Normandy'.[3] Until 1340 he was called 'King of England, Lord of Ireland, and Duke of Aquitaine'. In 1340, King Edward III assumed the title 'King of France' and thereafter was styled 'King of England and France, and Lord of Ireland'.

King Henry VIII (1509–47), second monarch of the Tudor dynasty, was styled, from 1542, 'King of England, France and

---

[2] Aquitaine by virtue of his wife's (Eleanor of Aquitaine) vast lands in France.
[3] British monarchs, however, are Dukes of Normandy as far as the Channel Islands are concerned.

The Royal Family from the Reign of Queen Victoria to June 1996

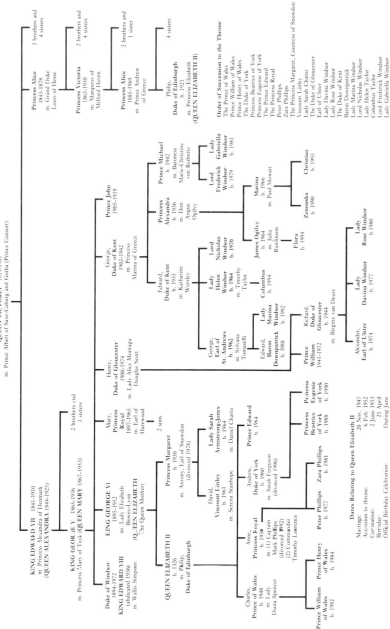

QUEEN VICTORIA 1819-1901
m. Prince Albert of Saxe-Coburg and Gotha (Prince Consort)

KING EDWARD VII 1841-1910
m. Princess Alexandra of Denmark
(QUEEN ALEXANDRA 1844-1925)

KING GEORGE V 1865-1936
m. Princess Mary of Teck (QUEEN MARY 1867-1953)

Princess Alice
1843-1878
m. Grand Duke
Louis of Hesse
3 brothers and 4 sisters

Princess Victoria
1863-1950
m. Marquess of
Milford Haven
2 brothers and 4 sisters

Princess Alice
1885-1969
m. Prince Andrew
of Greece
2 brothers and 1 sister

Philip,
Duke of Edinburgh
b. 1921
m. Princess Elizabeth
(QUEEN ELIZABETH II)
4 sisters

Duke of Windsor
1894-1972
KING EDWARD VIII
(abdicated 1936)
m. Lady
Wallis Simpson

2 brothers and 3 sisters

KING GEORGE VI
1895-1952
m. Lady Elizabeth
Bowes-Lyon
(QUEEN ELIZABETH
The Queen Mother)

Mary,
Princess
Royal
1897-1965
m. Earl of
Harewood
2 sons

Henry,
Duke of Gloucester
1900-1974
m. Lady Alice Montagu
Douglas Scott

Prince John
1905-1919

George,
Duke of Kent
1902-1942
m. Princess
Marina of Greece

Order of Succession to the Throne

The Prince of Wales
Prince William of Wales
Prince Henry of Wales
The Duke of York
Princess Beatrice of York
Princess Eugenie of York
The Prince Edward
The Princess Royal
Peter Phillips
Zara Phillips
The Princess Margaret, Countess of Snowdon
Viscount Linley
Lady Sarah Chatto
The Duke of Gloucester
Earl of Ulster
Lady Davina Windsor
Lady Rose Windsor
The Duke of Kent
Baron Downpatrick
Lord Nicholas Windsor
Lady Helen Taylor
Columbus Taylor
Lord Frederick Windsor
Lady Gabriella Windsor

QUEEN ELIZABETH II
b. 1926
m. Philip,
Duke of Edinburgh

Princess Margaret
b. 1930
m. Antony, Earl of Snowdon
(divorced 1978)

Edward,
Duke of Kent
b. 1935
m. Katharine
Worsley

Princess
Alexandra
b. 1936
m. Hon.
Angus
Ogilvy

Prince Michael
b. 1942
m. Baroness
Marie-Christine
von Reibnitz

Lady
Gabriella
Windsor
b. 1981

Lord
Frederick
Windsor
b. 1979

George,
Earl of
St. Andrews
b. 1962
m. Sylvana
Tomaselli

Lady
Helen
Windsor
b. 1964
m. Timothy
Taylor

Lord
Nicholas
Windsor
b. 1970

James Ogilvy
b. 1964
m. Julia
Rawlinson

Marina
b. 1966
m. Paul Mowatt

Edward,
Baron
Downpatrick
b. 1988

Lady
Marina
Windsor
b. 1992

Columbus
b. 1994

Flora
b. 1994

Zenouska
b. 1990

Christian
b. 1993

Richard,
Duke of
Gloucester
1941-1972
m. Birgitte van Deurs

Charles,
Prince of Wales
b. 1948
m. Lady
Diana Spencer

Anne,
Princess Royal
b. 1950
m. (1) Captain
Mark Phillips
(divorced 1992)
(2) Commander
Timothy Laurence

Andrew,
Duke of York
b. 1960
m. Sarah Ferguson
(divorced 1996)

Prince Edward
b. 1964

David,
Viscount Linley
b. 1961
m. Serena Stanhope

Lady Sarah
Armstrong-Jones
b. 1964
m. Daniel Chatto

Prince William
of Wales
b. 1982

Prince Henry
of Wales
b. 1984

Peter Phillips
b. 1977

Zara Phillips
b. 1981

Princess
Beatrice
of York
b. 1988

Princess
Eugenie
of York
b. 1990

Alexander,
Earl of Ulster
b. 1974

Lady
Davina Windsor
b. 1977

Lady
Rose Windsor
b. 1980

Dates Relating to Queen Elizabeth II

Marriage:	20 Nov. 1947
Accession to throne:	6 Feb. 1952
Coronation:	2 June 1953
Birthday:	21 April
Official Birthday Celebration	During June

Ireland, Defender of the Faith, and of the Church of England and also of Ireland, on Earth the Supreme Head'. He was also the first to be addressed as 'Your Majesty', which gradually displaced 'Your Highness' and 'Your Grace'. The title 'Defender of the Faith' was conferred on Henry VIII by Pope Leo X in 1521 in recognition of the King's book *Defence of the Seven Sacraments* asserting Catholic orthodoxy. It was not discontinued after the breach between Henry and the papacy in 1534. It has been assumed by all Henry's successors.

The late Stuart sovereigns were called 'King of England, Scotland, France and Ireland . . .'. After the Union of 1707, Queen Anne was known as 'Queen of Great Britain, France and Ireland. . .'. The early Hanoverians added 'Duke of Brunswick-Luneburg'. In 1801, after the Union of Great Britain and Ireland, King George III, and his successors, became 'of the United Kingdom of Great Britain and Ireland, King . . .'; the claim to France was finally dropped. In 1877 'Empress of India' was added to the titles of Queen Victoria. The style of King Edward VII (1901–10) mirrored the extension of Britain's overseas commitments: 'of the United Kingdom of Great Britain and Ireland, and of the British Dominions beyond the Seas, King, . . .Emperor of India'. In 1927 the royal style was changed to 'of Great Britain, Ireland and the British Dominions beyond the Seas. . .'. The title 'Emperor of India' was dropped by royal proclamation on 22 June 1948. The Royal Titles Act 1953 and the royal proclamation of 28 May 1953 settled the Queen's present style.

Regal Numerals
The Sovereign's regal numeral in England has been established from the beginning of the Norman dynasty in England in 1066.

The older, pre-Conquest, English kings are not taken into account. Thus, the three kings called Edward before 1066 (Edward the Elder, Edward the Martyr, and Edward the Confessor) are ignored and the numbering of Edwards begins with King Edward I (1272–1307).

The first King of England to use enumeration on documents was King Edward II (1307–27), although King Henry III (1216–72) had used 'Henricus III' on coinage issued during his reign.

In Scotland numerals started with King James IV (1488–1513), as evidenced by inscriptions on his coinage. The present custom is to use the lowest numeral not yet used in England or Scotland.

The Sovereign's Consort

There is no automatic title for the husband of a British Queen Regnant (see Appendix 1). The Queen's husband, His Royal Highness The Prince Philip, Duke of Edinburgh, has had his titles specially conferred on him by the Sovereign. He is the son of Prince Andrew of Greece and Denmark and his wife, the former Princess Alice of Battenberg. Princess Alice was the eldest daughter of Prince Louis of Battenberg, whose wife was Princess Victoria of Hesse, granddaughter of Queen Victoria. In 1947 Prince Philip renounced his Greek and Danish royal titles and became a British subject, under his mother's family name, Mountbatten. Just before his marriage to The Princess Elizabeth in the same year, King George VI created him Duke of Edinburgh, Earl of Merioneth and Baron Greenwich, and authorised his use of the prefix 'His Royal Highness'. In 1957 the Queen granted him the style and dignity of a Prince of the United Kingdom.

The consort of a British king is made royal by her marriage and called 'The Queen' during his lifetime. She is entitled for life to the prefix 'Her Majesty'. In late medieval and Tudor times the queen consort of England was called 'her highness' or 'her grace'. When there was again a queen consort after 1603, she shared the prefix 'Majesty'.

The Sovereign's Widow

In recent times the expression 'Queen Mother' has come into use for the widow of a British King and mother of the Sovereign.[4] Queen Alexandra was known as Queen Mother, and this is the title used by the mother of the present Sovereign, Queen Elizabeth The Queen Mother. The former Lady Elizabeth Bowes-Lyon is the youngest daughter of the 14th Earl of Strathmore and Kinghorne—two Scottish peerages created in the 17th century.

The widow of a king was also known as 'Queen Dowager' to differentiate her from the new consort or the new Queen Regnant—for example, Catherine of Braganza, widow of King Charles II (1660–85), and Adelaide of Saxe-Meiningen, widow of King William IV (1830–37), both without surviving children. The widow of King George V, mother of King Edward VIII and King George VI and grandmother of the present Queen, was always known, by her own wish, as Queen Mary.

Should a widowed queen remarry, she does not forfeit her royal status, title or privileges. The last to do so was the 'purposeful and elevated' Katherine Parr, sixth wife and widow of

[4] In his diary (5 January 1711) Sir David Hamilton, physician to Queen Anne, refers to Mary Beatrice of Modena, widow of King James II and Anne's exiled stepmother, as Queen Mother (*Diary of Sir David Hamilton*, ed. Philip Roberts, Oxford, 1975, p. 25).

Henry VIII ('Kateryn the Quene KP'—as she signed herself), who after Henry's death married Thomas Lord Seymour of Sudeley, uncle of her stepson, King Edward VI. Such was the esteem in which she was held that in 1544, during Henry's absence on campaign in France, she was appointed 'governor and protector of the realm'. She then signed herself 'Kateryn the Quene Regente KP', the only woman in English history to use this title.[5]

The Children of the Sovereign

The legitimate children of a Sovereign are automatically royal and entitled to be styled 'Royal Highness'. The sons are Princes and the daughters Princesses (see Appendix 2); wives of sons are also styled 'Royal Highness'. The eldest son of the Sovereign is automatically Duke of Cornwall in the peerage of England, and Duke of Rothesay, Earl of Carrick and Baron of Renfrew in the peerage of Scotland. He is also Lord of the Isles and Great Steward of Scotland. It is customary for him to be at some point created Prince of Wales and Earl of Chester. The Queen's eldest son, The Prince Charles, was given these titles in 1958. He was officially invested as Prince of Wales at Caernarfon Castle in 1968.

[5]   Catherine of Aragon, Henry's first wife, was proclaimed governor of the realm and captain-general of the forces while he was on campaign in northern France in 1513. Her organisational abilities contributed to the English victory over the Scots at Flodden. Caroline of Anspach, consort of King George II (1727–60), was appointed Guardian of the Realm (or Guardian of the Kingdom) in 1729, 1732, 1735 and 1736–37, during the King's absences in Hanover.
   In 1554 Marie de Guise, widow of King James V of Scots, was appointed Queen Regent of Scotland for her daughter Queen Mary, who was being brought up at the court of France. 'A crowne was putt upon hir head', wrote John Knox, 'als semlye a sight (yf men had eis) as to putt a sadill upoun the back of ane unruly kow'.

The wife of the Prince of Wales is the Princess of Wales. It has been incorrect to refer to the wife of Prince Charles, the former Lady Diana Spencer, as 'Princess Diana'.

The younger sons of the Sovereign are usually created dukes (see Appendix 2). The second son has usually been created Duke of York. The Queen's second son, The Prince Andrew, was created Duke of York in 1986 (with the subsidiary titles Earl of Inverness and Baron Killyleagh), before his marriage to Miss Sarah Ferguson. The Queen's youngest son is The Prince Edward.

The eldest daughter of the Sovereign has, at the Sovereign's discretion, customarily been given the title 'The Princess Royal'. The first to be so designated was Mary, eldest daughter of King Charles I, in 1642. The Princess Anne was created Princess Royal in 1987. The title, once given, belongs to the holder for life and can be held by only one person at a time.

The prefix 'The' before 'Prince' or 'Princess' (coming before a forename) is used only for the children of the Sovereign. The children of the sons of the Sovereign, and the eldest son of the eldest son of the Prince of Wales, have the right to be called Prince or Princess, with the prefix Royal Highness. The sons of The Prince and Princess of Wales are His Royal Highness Prince William of Wales and His Royal Highness Prince Henry of Wales.

The children of daughters of the Sovereign take their rank from their fathers. The mother's lineage does not make them royal or peers. The Princess Royal's children do not even have the courtesy titles given to the sons and daughters of peers (see p. 75) since their father does not possess a peerage.

With the exception of the eldest son of the eldest son of the Prince of Wales, the grandchildren of the Sovereign's sons are not born royal, and are only peers if they receive or inherit a peerage. Thus the elder son of the Duke of Kent (and great-grandson of George V), styled by courtesy Earl of St Andrews, is not a prince and will never be a royal duke, even on succeeding to his father's dukedom. The son of the Duke of Gloucester, styled by courtesy Earl of Ulster, is in a similar position. The children of Prince Michael of Kent, the Duke of Kent's brother, are styled 'Lord' and 'Lady' by courtesy although their father does not possess a dukedom or a marquessate (see p. 76). By Letters Patent (see p. 47) issued by George V in 1917 the grandchildren of the sons of the Sovereign (in direct male line) have the same style as the children of dukes.

The Use of Surnames

The name Plantagenet (from 'planta genista'—sprig of flowering broom) was adopted by Geoffrey of Anjou, father of Henry II, as his badge. It became the name of the English dynasty which began with Henry II in 1154 and ended with King Richard III (1483–85), and included the house of Lancaster and the house of York. Its first recorded use as a surname was in 1448, by Richard, Duke of York, father of King Edward IV and of Richard III. The two following dynasties in England bore surnames— Tudor (originally a Welsh forename[6]) and Stuart, from the Stuarts' hereditary office of High Steward of Scotland. It has been said that the house of Hanover and the house of Saxe-Coburg and Gotha (family of the husband of Queen Victoria) were of such ancient stock that they did not possess a surname. In 1917 George V proclaimed that the name of Windsor should be borne by the royal house, and that the use of all German names and

[6] Henry VII's great-grandfather was Maredudd (Meredith) ap Tudor. The Welsh did not have surnames in medieval times and sons bore the qualification 'ap', meaning 'son of'.

titles should cease. The royal family is thus styled and known as the House and Family of Windsor. In 1960 the Queen provided that those of her descendants through the male line who were not entitled to the style of Royal Highness, or Prince or Princess, should use the surname Mountbatten-Windsor, a compound of her husband's surname and that of the royal house.

The Royal Household

Great Officers of State

The Royal Household of England was originally the centre of the system of government. The leading dignitaries of the palace— the Sovereign's closest advisers—were also the principal administrators of the State. With the development of ministerial responsibility for executive acts, many leading members of the original Royal Household—the Lord Chancellor, the Lord President of the Council, the Lord Privy Seal and the Secretary of State (an office now divided between a number of ministers)— became members of the political administration and ceased to be involved in household duties. The functions of the Lord High Treasurer are now carried out by the Lords Commissioners of the Treasury, who are government Whips in the House of Commons. The offices of Lord High Steward and Lord High Constable of England are now granted only for the single day of a coronation. While no great officer of State retains household functions, two (the Lord Great Chamberlain of England and the Earl Marshal of England) retain duties in connection with royal ceremonial.

Some of the offices, especially those of historical significance, are described below.

Lord Great Chamberlain of England
The office of Lord Great Chamberlain dates back to the reign of King Henry I (1100–35). In 1539, Thomas Cromwell, Henry

VIII's chief minister, stepped into the job, intending to turn it into an effective headship of all the royal household, but his fall from power prevented his scheme from being fully realised.

The office has since become hereditary and its duties purely ceremonial. It belongs jointly to three families: those of the Marquess of Cholmondeley, the Marquess of Lincolnshire, and the Earl of Ancaster. The heads of these families hold office in turn, by agreement, each for the duration of a reign. The present holder is the 7th Marquess of Cholmondeley; the present heads of the other two families are Lord Carrington (representing the late Marquess of Lincolnshire)[7] and Baroness Willoughby de Eresby (representing the late Earl of Ancaster)[8].

Few ancient duties now attach to the office, but the holder is responsible for the arrangements when the Sovereign attends Parliament. He plays an important role at the coronation, when his duties include presenting the Golden Spurs, fastening the clasps of the imperial mantle after investiture, and dressing the Sovereign in purple robes before the procession out of the Abbey.

Since each Lord Great Chamberlain takes office immediately a new reign begins, he has to help arrange for the Lying in State of the late monarch in Westminster Hall.

Earl Marshal of England
The office of Earl Marshal of England also originated in the

---

[7] Charles Robert Carington (1843–1928), 3rd Baron Carrington, created Viscount Wendover and Earl Carrington in 1895 and Marquess of Lincolnshire in 1912, was joint hereditary Lord Great Chamberlain for the reign of George V. The present 6th Lord Carrington is his great-nephew.

[8] Gilbert James Heathcote-Drummond-Willoughby, 3rd Earl of Ancaster and 26th Baron Willoughby de Eresby (1907–83), was joint hereditary Lord Great Chamberlain for the reign of George VI. His daughter, and only surviving child, succeeded to the barony.

reign of Henry I. It has been hereditary in the family of the Duke of Norfolk since 1672, when it was granted to Henry Howard, future 6th Duke. The Earl Marshal has certain responsibilities for the Royal Heralds (see p. 28) and for the arrangements for the Sovereign's coronation, the State funeral of the Sovereign, and other State occasions, such as the opening of Parliament.

The coronation of George III and Queen Charlotte in 1761 was marred by the incompetence of the deputy Earl Marshal, Thomas Howard, 2nd Earl of Effingham (c 1714–1763), 'whose repeated blunders caused endless confusion and general amusement'. In Westminster Hall, no chairs of state had been provided for the King and Queen; the canopy was missing altogether; the sword of state had been forgotten—the Lord Mayor's had to be borrowed for the occasion. When the King complained of these omissions, 'It is true, Sir', was Effingham's reply, 'that there has been some neglect, but I have taken care that the next coronation shall be regulated in the exactest manner possible'.

Officers of the Royal Household

Certain offices have become obsolete with time[9] and a few have been created comparatively recently to meet modern requirements. A number, however, have been retained since Plantagenet

[9] Thus the Groom of the Stole once ranked next below the Vice-Chamberlain of the Household. The office's origins went back to medieval times. In the 15th century the King's pewter chamber pot, enclosed in a stool or box, elaborately upholstered or trimmed, was first entrusted to a Yeoman, and then to a Groom. His responsibilities multiplied. In the reign of James I (1603–25) he emerged as First Gentleman of the Bedchamber. In the reign of Charles I (1625–49) he helped dress the King in the morning, rode in the royal coach, attended as cupbearer when the King dined privately or with the Queen, and supervised the Gentlemen and grooms of the Bedchamber. He had rights to the leftovers after the King had dined. In the Household ordinances of 1661 the Groom of the Stole 'may wear a gold key in a blue ribbon as a badge of his office'.

In 1837, at the accession of Queen Victoria, the office was abolished. The Chancellor of the Exchequer, Thomas Spring-Rice, announced in Parliament that the chief office of the Bedchamber would remain unfilled. The announcement brought 'a laugh'.

and Tudor times, although the duties attached to them are now very different.

Lord Steward

For centuries the Lord Steward, the first dignitary of the Court, was responsible for the functioning of the Palace—Hall, kitchens, accounting and household management, with various domestic offices, including bakehouse, wafery, scaldinghouse, accatery and saucery—and managed the catering arrangements for State banquets, Courts, and all other forms of royal entertaining, together with the payment of all Household expenses. He presided over the Board of Green Cloth, a judicial body which formerly supervised the work and finances of the department. Nowadays these functions are carried out by the department of the Master of the Household, who is a permanent officer, while the Board of Green Cloth exists only as licensing authority for premises within a prescribed area around Buckingham Palace. The Lord Steward, appointed by the Sovereign, still retains the titular authority and, on ceremonial occasions, bears a white staff as an emblem of his position.

Treasurer, Comptroller and Vice-Chamberlain

The offices of Treasurer of the Household, Comptroller of the Household and Vice-Chamberlain of the Household are now political appointments—government Whips in the House of Commons—and change with a change of government.

In medieval times Treasurer and Comptroller[10] ranked above

[10] Among holders of the office was Sir Robert Rochester (c 1494–1557), Comptroller of the Royal Household 1553–57, and one of Mary I's most intimate and trusted counsellors. He, the Vice-Chamberlain and the Master of the Horse, 'governed access to her apartments and her person . . . guarded her security and were in every way the chief figures of her court'.

the Cofferer, who ran the counting house. With the Lord Steward and the Cofferer and his clerks, they sat as 'the board of doom . . . at the Green Cloth in the counting house as recorders and witnesses to the truth'.

Lord Chamberlain

The Lord Chamberlain, formerly the second dignitary of the Court, is now the senior member of the Household, and carries a white staff and wears a golden key on ceremonial occasions as a symbol of his office. He oversees the conduct of business of the Household and is involved in all senior appointments to it. He also undertakes ceremonial duties, is Chancellor of the Royal Victorian Order (see p. 97), and is the Queen's emissary to the House of Lords.

In late medieval times he and his department 'staged public ceremony and provided the king's private service'. It presided over such agencies as the Jewel House and such personnel as the Minstrels and Trumpeters. The Tudor kings sought more privacy in more retired apartments, called the Privy Chamber,[11] and the royal household became divided into three parts: Household, Chamber, and Privy Chamber. After a period of eclipse under Henry VII and Henry VIII, under Queen Elizabeth I the office of Lord Chamberlain recovered its importance. It was given new responsibilities as head of the Privy Chamber and of the household 'above stairs'. The Lord Chamberlain also regained his influence as organiser of royal progresses and of the allocation of lodgings at court.

[11] In medieval times the Chamber had been the King's private apartment—one room in which he slept, ate, and conducted most of his public business and all of his private. At Westminster it was 80 feet long, 26 feet wide and more than 30 feet high. It became the Parliament chamber. During the 14th and 15th centuries, the one-room chamber was replaced by a suite of three rooms: Guard Chamber, Presence Chamber, with throne and canopy, and Privy Chamber.

The Comptroller of the Lord Chamberlain's Office is in charge of the work of the Office, which is responsible for the organisation of State visits to the Queen, the Queen's ceremonial engagements, such as investitures and garden parties, and the ceremonial on major occasions such as royal weddings and royal funerals. The Office co-ordinates arrangements for the Queen to be represented at funerals and memorial services. It advises on matters of precedence, styles and titles, dress, flying of flags, gun salutes, mourning and other ceremonial questions. The Lord Chamberlain's Office is also responsible for supervising applications for Royal Warrants of Appointment from businesses, and the commercial use of royal photographs and royal emblems.

The Office oversees the Household duties of the Ecclesiastical Household, the Medical Household, the Bodyguards and certain ceremonial appointments such as Gentlemen Ushers and Pages of Honour. It is also responsible for the Lords-in-Waiting, the Queen's Bargemaster and the Royal Watermen, the Crown Jewels and the Queen's Swans.

Under the aegis of the Lord Chamberlain's Office come the Marshal of the Diplomatic Corps, who has responsibility for relations between the diplomatic heads of Mission in London and Buckingham Palace over ceremonial, formal and social matters; and the Secretary of the Central Chancery of the Orders of Knighthood, who administers the Orders of Chivalry (but not the Order of the Thistle, nor, in certain respects, the Order of the Garter and the Order of Merit) and their records, makes arrangements for recipients at investitures and distribution of insignia, and ensures proper public notification of awards through the *London Gazette*. The Secretary of the Central Chancery also carries out certain duties as Assistant Comptroller.

The Ecclesiastical Household in England consists of the Clerk of the Closet, usually a bishop, whose traditional duty was 'to attend at the right hand of the Sovereign in the Royal Closet during Divine Service to resolve such doubts as may arise concerning spiritual matters'; the Deputy Clerk of the Closet; the Dean and Sub-Dean of the Chapels Royal; and domestic chaplains, chaplains of the Chapels Royal, priests-in-ordinary and chaplains to the Queen. The latter posts, known collectively as the College of Chaplains, are honorific appointments. These chaplains have a rota of attendance to preach at royal chapels.

Master of the Horse

The Master of the Horse is the third dignitary of the Court. In Charles II's reign the Lord Chamberlain occupied 40 rooms at Whitehall, the Comptroller 19 and the Master of the Horse 20. He had and has charge of the Sovereign's stables, and is responsible for providing the horses, carriages and motor cars required for processions and for the daily needs of the royal family. His day-to-day duties are carried out by his deputy—the Chief (or Crown) Equerry. The Master of the Horse rides immediately behind the Sovereign in State processions.

Most equerries of the Household—regular, extra or honorary—are officers of the armed services. There are usually two regular equerries, one of whom is always in waiting upon the Sovereign.

Keeper of the Privy Purse and Treasurer to the Sovereign

The Keeper of the Privy Purse and Treasurer to the Sovereign deals with payments made from the Sovereign's private resources as well as official expenditure, and the payment of salaries and wages to the Sovereign's officers and servants. Under Henry VII, while the Treasurer had almost full control over the Crown's finances, the King's privy purse was kept by the Groom of the Stole. In 1495 Henry VII's Groom, Hugh Denys, was paying alms and royal gambling debts, and giving tips and handling the King's shopping expenses—at about £200–500 a year all told.

At the head of the Royal Almonry, part of the same department, is the Lord High Almoner—an ecclesiastical appointment usually held by a bishop—who in former times was responsible for the Sovereign's almsgiving.

The Private Secretary
Each Sovereign has, since the latter half of the 19th century, appointed his or her own Private Secretary. Queen Victoria's first official appointment was Lieutenant General the Hon. Charles Grey (1804–70) in 1867. The longest-serving holder of the office has been Sir Arthur Bigge (from 1911 Lord Stamfordham; 1849–1931) who worked for Queen Victoria and for King George V for a total of 27 years. The Private Secretary, helped by a Deputy and an Assistant Private Secretary, deals with all the correspondence between the Queen and her ministers, whether of the British or other Commonwealth Governments. Government appointments for which the Queen's approval is required go to the Queen through her Private Secretary. The Private Secretary is also concerned with the Queen's speeches, messages and private papers, and is responsible for her engagements, both in Britain and overseas; for the office of the Press Secretary; and for the royal archives.

The Press Office, which has undergone considerable expansion in recent years, deals with all press, broadcasting and related matters on behalf of the Queen, the Duke of Edinburgh and other members of the Royal Family.[12]

Royal Collection Department

In 1625 Charles I created the post of 'Overseer or Surveyor of all our pictures', first held by Abraham van der Doordt. The King was a renowned connoisseur, had inherited the art treasures of his mother, Anne of Denmark, and his brother Henry Prince of Wales (1594–1612), and went on to assemble the finest collection in Christendom. He owned works by Mantegna, Raphael and Titian and was patron of the Netherlandish painters Daniel Mytens, Peter Paul Rubens, and Anthony van Dyck. Most of his collection was sold or otherwise dispersed under the Commonwealth.[13] The present Royal Collection owes much to the keenness of some of Charles's successors. Charles II, for example, reacquired as much of what had been his father's as he could and was presented with 27 paintings by Dutch masters by the government of the States General at the beginning of his reign. Samuel Pepys tells us that the Gallery containing the King's paintings at Whitehall was always open to gentlemen.

Over 600 of the drawings of Leonardo da Vinci, now in the

---

[12] The Court Newsman, from the reign of George III, distributed the *Court Circular* (officially describing royal activities) to the daily papers. Queen Victoria's Court Newsman attended at Buckingham Palace twice a day when the Queen was in London, and once a day when she was away from the capital— for a salary of £45, reduced in 1909 to £20. A full-time Press Secretary was appointed in 1918 and again, after the office had been taken over by the Assistant Private Secretary in 1931, in 1944.

[13] A Rembrandt went for £5. Francis Tryon, a London merchant, bought several pictures, in hope of presenting them one day to Charles II, including 'one raerre peese of the present King, the Princes Royall, the Duek of Yarcke, the Prinses Elizabett holding haer Suster the Prinsesse Anna upan haer lap, all in one peese, of Sir Antonio V'Dike'.

Royal Library, came into the Royal Collection in the 17th century, as did the 81 portrait drawings by Hans Holbein of prominent figures at the court of Henry VIII. In the early 1760s George III bought the prize collection of Joseph Smith, British consul at Venice, and the Albani collection, obtained for him in Rome by James Adam. He also rescued (for 500 guineas) Van Dyck's painting of the Children of Charles I (see above), now at Windsor.[14] George IV, another royal connoisseur, built up an unrivalled display of French works of art, and added many fine Dutch paintings to the collection.

The Director of the Royal Collection today co-ordinates the work of the Surveyor of The Queen's Pictures, the Surveyor of The Queen's Works of Art and the Librarian of the Royal Library. The Director is appointed to hold this post concurrently with one of these three positions.

The Surveyor of The Queen's Pictures is responsible for the Royal Collection of pictures and miniatures; this includes supervising the conservation of the pictures and their hanging and security, initiating and assisting research into the history of the Royal Collection, and making as large a part as possible of the collection accessible to the public either by display in the State Rooms and Apartments of palaces open to the public, and in the Queen's Gallery, or by loans to exhibitions. The Surveyor also advises members of the royal family on their private collections. The Surveyor of The Queen's Works of Art has similar responsibilities relating to the decorative arts. The Librarian of the Royal Library is responsible for maintaining all the items held within the Royal Library, including the watercolours, prints and drawings in the Print Room at Windsor Castle. He has the same

[14] James II is said to have given it, at an inappropriate moment, to his mistress, Catherine Sedley, Countess of Dorchester. George III got it back from her heirs.

responsibilities as his colleagues in respect of conservation, display and study of the collections in his care.

Ladies-in-Waiting

The Mistress of the Robes is the senior lady of the Queen's Household, and is usually a duchess. She is responsible for arranging the rota for the ladies-in-waiting and is in attendance on the Queen on State occasions, sometimes accompanying her on other important visits.

Mary I's mistress of the robes, Susan Clarentius (Susan White, Mrs Tonge, called Clarentius because her husband had been Clarenceux, King of Arms), although close to the Queen, was not politically influential.[15] One of Elizabeth I's mistresses of the robes, Mary Shelton, Lady Scudamore, was not regarded as influential either. The Queen, it was reported at the beginning of her reign, resolved not to discuss business with her ladies. One of Lady Scudamore's relations regretted her lack of using influence advantageously: 'I am afraid that your lordship is not likely to hear in haste from my cousin Scudamore . . . She is one that is wont to delay more than needs and loseth many a tide for the taking . . .'[16] Queen Anne's mistress of the robes, Groom of the Stole and Keeper of the Privy Purse, Sarah Churchill Duchess of Marlborough, had great influence, which was, however, waning

[15] Although, according to the imperial ambassador, she supported the Queen's marriage with Philip of Spain 'to the uttermost'. It is to her that Mary said, after the fall of Calais in January 1558: 'when I am dead and opened you shall find Calais lying in my heart'.

[16] David Starkey and others, *The English Court: from the Wars of the Roses to the Civil War* (quoting Shrewsbury MS 707, folio 221 in Lambeth Palace Library), pp. 160–1. Under Elizabeth I the Chief Gentlewoman of the Privy Chamber was the keeper of the Queen's close-stools and looked after her jewellery. The office was distinct from that of Mistress of the Robes. The latter oversaw delivery of fabrics and finished clothes for the Queen.

before her bitterly contested dismissal in 1711.[17] Until well into the reign of Queen Victoria the post changed hands with the government of the day. Nowadays the appointment has no political significance, and the Queen appoints whom she pleases (see Appendix 3).

There are today two Ladies of the Bedchamber, always peeresses, who attend the Queen on important public occasions, but do not go into waiting regularly. An extra Lady of the Bedchamber is also occasionally called upon to attend the Queen. There are four Women of the Bedchamber, who, in turn, for a fortnight at a time, attend the Queen on all public and semi-private engagements, make her personal arrangements, do shopping and make enquiries about people who are ill. They also deal with some of the Queen's correspondence—answering most of the letters written to her by children. There are five extra Women of the Bedchamber who are in waiting occasionally.

Other Royal Households

Queen Elizabeth The Queen Mother's household is headed by her Lord Chamberlain. There are also the Comptroller, Private Secretary, Treasurer, Equerries, Ladies of the Bedchamber and Women of the Bedchamber.[18]

Other members of the royal family have their own, smaller, households.

---

[17] The Duchess's final, and stormy, interview with the Queen took place on 6 April 1710. 'The Queen also told me', wrote Sir David Hamilton (5 January 1711), 'that when the Duchess left her, she said, that God would punish her either in this world, or in the next for what she had done to her this day'. Not until 18 January 1711 was Sarah's removal formally completed (*Diary of Sir David Hamilton*, p. 25).

[18] The post of Mistress of the Robes in the Queen Mother's household has not lately been filled.

Great Officers of State of Scotland

Those great officers of State of Scotland who had a place in Parliament by virtue of their office were, and are, called 'Lord'—for example, the Lord High Chancellor, the Lord High Treasurer and the Lord Privy Seal. They, together with the Earl Marischal of Scotland, sat in the places allotted to their offices, and not among the peers (see p. 37). Many of the holders of these offices were peers, but they did not sit or vote as peers, but as great officers. Those who did not sit in Parliament as such were perhaps not all styled 'Lord'—for example, the Great Steward and the Master of the Household, who sat in Parliament as the Duke of Rothesay and the Earl of Argyll.

The great officers today are the Great Steward of Scotland, the Keeper of the Great Seal (the Secretary of State for Scotland), the Lord High Constable, the Master of the Household, the Lord Justice-General, the Lord Clerk Register, the Lord Advocate, the Lord Justice Clerk and the Lord Lyon King of Arms (see p. 29). Although not in former times a great officer, the role of Solicitor General for Scotland has developed since 1707 and his office is now regarded as important and significant.

The office of Great Steward of Scotland is held by The Prince Charles, Duke of Rothesay. It has been the custom to appoint a deputy for ceremonial occasions such as coronations.[19] The hereditary Lord High Constable of Scotland is the Earl of Erroll; the hereditary Master of the Household in Scotland is the

---

[19] The last coronation in Scotland was that of Charles II, at Scone on New Year's Day 1651. After that the Scottish crown jewels, 'The Honours of Scotland', Sceptre (1494), Sword of State (1507), and remodelled Crown (1540), were hidden from the English invaders under Oliver Cromwell. In 1707 they were consigned to an oak chest in Edinburgh Castle, until they were rediscovered, thanks to Walter Scott, in 1818.

Duke of Argyll; the hereditary Bearer of the Royal Banner of Scotland is the Earl of Dundee; and the hereditary Bearer of the Scottish National Flag is the Earl of Lauderdale.

Kings, Heralds and Pursuivants of Arms

England and Wales

The College of Arms in England and Wales is a corporation of 13 members—three Kings of Arms; six Heralds; and four Pursuivants. All are members of the Royal Household, appointed by the Queen, on the nomination of the Earl Marshal. The history of the Heralds as members of the Household goes back to the 13th century, but they were not constituted into a corporation until 1484, by Richard III. The present corporation dates from 1555, when Mary I granted it a new charter and Derby House, on the site of the present college building in London.

The Kings of Arms are Garter, Clarenceux, and Norroy and Ulster. The office of Ulster King of Arms was transferred from Dublin to London, and united with Norroy, in 1943. Garter was created in 1415 by King Henry V. He is both King of Arms of the Most Noble Order of the Garter and Principal King of English Arms. He is responsible to the Earl Marshal for the conduct of the ceremonial introduction of a peer in the House of Lords. Clarenceux and Norroy were constituted by the time of Edward III, the province of the former comprising all land to the south, and of the latter all land to the north, of the river Trent. (Clarenceux is named from the domains of the Earls of Clare; Norroy is derived from Norveis Roy—'King of the Northmen'.) The Kings of Arms, with royal authority, grant coats of arms by Letters Patent, in obedience to warrants from the Earl Marshal.

The six Heralds are Windsor, Chester, Lancaster, York, Richmond and Somerset, who take precedence according to seniority in office. Some say that the latter five are named from places which have been the styles of the Sovereign's younger sons: for instance, Lancaster from John of Gaunt, Duke of Lancaster, fourth son of Edward III; York from Edmund of Langley, Duke of York, fifth son of Edward III; and Somerset from Henry Fitzroy, Duke of Richmond and Somerset (1519–36), natural son of Henry VIII and Elizabeth Blount.

The four Pursuivants are Rouge Croix, Bluemantle, Rouge Dragon and Portcullis. Rouge Croix was instituted by Henry V (from the red cross of St George); Bluemantle's name is from the blue of the mantles worn by Knights of the Garter; Rouge Dragon and Portcullis were created (in 1485 and c 1490–99 respectively) by King Henry VII, the former being named from the dragon device of the Welsh princes (a tribute to the King's Welsh ancestry) and the latter from the King's own badge. Occasionally Heralds Extraordinary and Pursuivants Extraordinary are appointed.

In addition to verifying and recording arms and genealogies, the Kings of Arms, Heralds and Pursuivants attend the Sovereign on ceremonial occasions such as coronations, State funerals, State openings of Parliament and ceremonies connected with the Order of the Garter.

Scotland

In Scotland armorial functions are performed by the Lord Lyon King of Arms, an important officer of State, who with the other Scottish officers of Arms has been described as one of the Sovereign's 'familiar daylie servitors'. From the beginning of the 16th century the Court of the Lord Lyon has operated as one of the Courts of Law in Scotland, and since 1542 no Grant of Arms has been made by the Sovereign, but only by the Lord Lyon. The Lord Lyon is responsible for the preparation, conduct and record of State, royal and public ceremonial, and the making of royal proclamations, in addition to the granting of armorial bearings. He is appointed by the Sovereign and in turn appoints the other officers of Arms. There has been a Lyon since the 14th century.

Until 1867 there were six Heralds and six Pursuivants in Scotland, but following an Act of Parliament, these were reduced to three Heralds and three Pursuivants. There are thus six offices from which a Herald or Pursuivant respectively may take a title. The six Heralds are Albany, Islay, Marchmont, Ross, Rothesay and Snowdoun. Albany is first mentioned in 1401, an office probably being instituted on the creation of Robert Stewart, son of King Robert II (1371–90), as Duke of Albany in 1398, the same year that the dukedom of Rothesay was conferred on David, eldest son of King Robert III (1390–1406). The titles of Marchmont and Snowdoun are derived from royal castles, Snowdoun being the old name for Stirling Castle. The six Pursuivancies are Bute, Carrick, Dingwall, Kintyre, Ormond and Unicorn. The title 'Unicorn' is derived from the royal badge, while Carrick is derived from the earldom of Carrick held by King Robert the Bruce (1306–29) before his succession to the Crown. There are, in addition to the Ordinary offices, a number of Extraordinary offices which may be conferred.

The Lord Lyon King of Arms determines the right to armorial bearings both judicially and administratively, and his judicial decision may be appealed to the Court of Session and ultimately to the Judicial Committee of the House of Lords.

Within the Court, the Lord Lyon is assisted by the Lyon Clerk and Keeper of the Records, whose function it is to organise the administrative matters within the Court and give effect to the Warrants and Interlocutors of the Lord Lyon.

The Lord Lyon King of Arms, together with the Heralds and Pursuivants, attends the Sovereign on ceremonial occasions in Scotland, and at ceremonies in connection with the Order of the Thistle. He also attends on the Lord High Commissioner (see p. 82) and is present on other ceremonial occasions.

The Peerage: Categories and Degrees

The term 'baron' originally meant one who held land direct from the King. All the barons being equal in this respect, the word 'peers' (from Latin *par*, equal) could be applied to them and this is the origin of the term. Because the possession of land implied both wealth and command of manpower, the King of England made a practice of summoning the leading barons, including the earls (then an office rather than a status), when he called the most important people in the kingdom to his Great Council. Later the practice grew up of asking the shires and boroughs to send representatives also, and eventually two bodies emerged, the House of Lords, consisting of those who attended in response to an individual summons, and the House of Commons, containing members attending in a representative capacity, which, together with the King, made up the Parliament. Lords and Commons began to be regarded as separate during the reign of King Richard II (1377–99) and to sit separately in the 15th century.

Over the years the selection of individuals, which at first varied from one Parliament to the next, fell into a repetitive pattern based on precedent and so in effect hereditary, and a peer came to mean a person with a recognised right to a summons to the House of Lords. (Royal discretion in the issue of Writs of Summons to sit as peers in the House of Lords was not, however, finally declared unlawful until 1626.) Those who did not secure a place on the list ceased to be referred to as 'peers', and 'baron' came to mean a peer of the lowest degree.

There is no tradition of a closed caste of hereditary nobility in any of the countries which make up Britain. Peers could and did marry commoners if they wished, and fresh peerages were conferred from time to time by the Sovereign on anyone he or she wished to reward. Except in certain cases which will be discussed below, the title has normally come to pass to the eldest son. Only the current peer and his wife, and widows of dead peers, and peeresses in their own right, were considered noblemen and women. Their children were not automatically peers, though their noble origins were reflected in their position in the order of social precedence, determined partly by statute or Royal Warrant, but in larger measure by ancient custom and usage, and in the application to them of courtesy titles (see p. 75).

Indeed, the status of any descendant of a noble house who was not a peer ultimately depended as much on his or her own attributes and achievements as on lineage. Whereas on the continent of Europe 'nobility' was sharply defined and possessed important legal and fiscal privileges, in England 'gentility'—a gentleman is the lowest class in the order of precedence—was frequently only a question of reputation and esteem.

The peerage in Scotland has a number of features, attributable to the circumstances of Scottish social and legal development, which are more like the practice found upon the continent of Europe. An important difference from England is that in many cases the first barons were originally tribal chiefs and the individual peerage has been regarded as an honour of interest to all those of his blood and name, whom he in a sense represents, rather than as the personal privilege of the peer himself.[20]

In medieval times the grant of a new peerage used to be accompanied by a grant of land if the new peer would otherwise have inadequate means to support his new dignity. Nowadays, the grant of a new peerage confers no material advantages, but is a symbol of public recognition of people who have given distinguished service to the State and community in some walk of life; it also enables them to contribute to the work of Parliament through their membership of the House of Lords, where they receive expenses within specified limits for costs incurred in attending the House.

There was no separate peerage in Wales. The lands of the ancient Welsh aristocracy (*bonheddig*—men with pedigrees) were split up repeatedly between brothers and dwindled to very small units. Henry VIII (himself of Welsh descent) imposed primogeniture. By the 18th century a Welsh landed gentry had become established and Welshmen held peerages and baronetcies (see p. 85) of England and Great Britain.

---

[20] At the Union of Scotland and England in 1707, three Scottish lords, Borthwick, Colville of Culross and Somerville, did not assume their titles because they were so hard up. John Keith, 3rd Earl of Kintore (d. 1758) held the sinecure office of Knight Marischal and received a government salary. But, he wrote: 'I must let you know that my affairs having fallen into disorder I was oblidged to consent to a voluntary sequestration of my estate, and to put it under the manadgement of trustees for the payment of my creditors, so that att present I draw not a shilling from it, and have nothing to depend on for the subsistence of my family but the office I enjoy by the bounty of the Crown ... if I should acte any part that might give offence to the administration it would ruin me'. Royal Commission on Historical Manuscripts, Ninth Report (London 1883–84), part ii, 229. Quoted in John Stuart Shaw, *The Management of Scottish Society 1707–1764* (Edinburgh, 1983), pp. 2, 13.

Categories of Peerage

There are five categories of peerage in order of precedence: peerages of England, created before the union with Scotland of 1707; peerages of Scotland, created before the union with England; peerages of Ireland; peerages of Great Britain, created after the union between England and Scotland, but before the end of 1801—after the union with Ireland in July 1800; and peerages of the United Kingdom, created since the union with Ireland.

England

The peerage of England is the senior peerage. None of the earliest medieval peerages, deriving from Writ of Summons or created by Letters Patent, have survived in unbroken succession through the male line. Most became extinct or dormant or fell into abeyance (see p. 49) during the 15th and later centuries. Some of their holders lost their titles by attainder[21] during the Wars of the Roses (for backing the wrong side); others were killed in battle. The Yorkist and Tudor monarchs broke several ancient houses by attainder or by having their senior representatives executed. By 1485, when Henry VII became King, with what was regarded as a tenuous claim, few great noble houses had survived, thus making it easier for Henry to consolidate his position. The execution of Edward Stafford, Duke of Buckingham, at the hands of Henry VIII in 1521 removed one of the few surviving possible rivals for the Tudor crown. There were 42 lay

---

[21] Attainder involved forfeiture of peerage, and all property, and 'corruption of blood', so that the condemned could neither transmit nor inherit property or peerage. It also meant extinction of all civil rights. The peerage could be restored only by Act of Parliament or due course of law.

peers in England when Henry VIII came to the throne in 1509.[22] Only 50 (two dukes, one marquess, 15 earls and 32 barons) were summoned to the Parliament he called in 1539.

Some early peerages were revived in later centuries. For example, the earldom of Devon, in the family of Courtenay since 1335, was forfeited in 1471, when the 8th earl was attainted. The title was revived in 1485 for Edward Courtenay, who died in 1509, under a cloud, for his son and heir, William, had been attainted. In 1511 Henry VIII forgave William and created him Earl of Devon, but he died a month later. In 1525 the 2nd earl of the new creation was made Marquess of Exeter, only to be attainted before execution in 1539. In 1553 Mary I created the earldom again for his son, who died childless in 1556. The remainder (see p. 41), however, was to all his male heirs—that is, male members of his wider family. The peerage remained dormant until 1831, when another branch of Courtenays established their right to his earldom. In 1916 the ancient baronies of Burgh, Dudley, Strabolgi and Wharton were called out of abeyance on the same day (see p. 50).

A very few English peerages created by Letters Patent which exist today date from the 15th century. Some date from the 16th century, even though the Tudors were sparing in their creation of peers (see above). Most date from the 17th century. The holders of a number of them possess titles of a higher grade in another peerage category (see p. 35). Thus the Duke of Manchester (cr. 1719; peerage of Great Britain) is also Earl of

---

[22] In June 1525 Sir John Arundell of Lanherne in Cornwall wrote to decline the King's offer (at short notice) of a barony. 'If his grace knew the moche unworthenes and lake of abilitie in me many waies, as well for to receve suche honnour as to the contynuall maintenaunce of the same to his honnour and my poor honeste, I know well his grace wuld not offere hit to me'. Helen Miller, *Henry VIII and the English Nobility* (Oxford, 1986), p. 21.

Manchester (cr. 1626), Viscount Mandeville and Baron Montagu (cr. 1620) in the peerage of England.

Scotland

In the kingdom of Scotland the three estates of nobles, Commissioners of the Shires, and Commissioners of the Burghs, which comprised the Parliament, sat together in one house. Noble titles were considered hereditary.

In the Scottish peerage the equivalent of a baron in England is termed a Lord of Parliament. The word 'baron' in Scotland relates to feudal barons, survival of a system which lasted longer in Scotland than in England. They are landed proprietors who do not possess any peerage title conferred by the Sovereign (see p. 120).

Most Scottish peerages date from the 17th century, although some survive from medieval times. The earldom of Mar (cr. c 1115) is the oldest peerage of all. The earldom of Crawford dates from 1398; other earldoms from the 15th century (see p. 57); and various lordships from the same period. (There are today some 19 Scottish peerages created before 1600.) In 1707 the Scottish peerage numbered 154, compared with 190 English peers.

After the Union 16 Scottish peers were to be elected by their fellow peers to sit as representatives of the Scots peerage in the House of Lords in London for the duration of each Parliament. In 1782 the principle was established that a Scottish peer who also held a peerage of Great Britain could sit in the House of Lords as a peer of Great Britain (see p. 40).

Unlike Irish peers (see p. 39), those Scottish peers not elected to the Lords did not enjoy the right to stand for election to the House of Commons. The Peerage Act 1963, however, entitled all

Scottish peers to sit in the House of Lords.

Ireland
The first Parliament of Ireland, called by Ireland's Anglo-Norman rulers in Dublin, is said to have been held in 1264. By 1310 a Parliament representative of the main temporal and spiritual interests had been established. In the 15th century the lay magnates were said to be 'eagerly seeking parliamentary peerages and jealous of their precedence'. By the end of the 15th century, the number of temporal peers had dwindled to 15, reflecting the difficulty the central government had in trying to establish control over the country. A Parliament of two separate houses was confirmed in 1537. In 1535, it was reported, Henry VIII was planning to make barons in Ireland 'for the encrese of the number of temperal lordes of his parlament there'.

Henry VIII conferred peerages on native Irish Chiefs: Con O'Neill, Chief of the O'Neills in Ulster, was created Earl of Tyrone and Baron Dungannon in 1542; Murrough, Chief of Clan O'Brien, was created Earl of Thomond and Baron Inchiquin in 1543.

The majority of Irish peerages were created in the 18th century and Irish peers, mainly representing Anglo-Irish landed interests, were entitled to sit in the Irish House of Lords in Dublin, but not in its equivalent in London. Irish peerages could be given to Englishmen who, it was said, did not merit an English or a Great Britain dignity, and their designations were not necessarily Irish (for example, Earl of Mexborough, Lord Kensington and Lord Teignmouth).

The Union with Ireland Act 1800 terminated the Parliament of Ireland and provided that the Irish peers should elect 28 of their number to sit, for life, as their representatives in the House of Lords in London. (The total number of Irish peers was to be maintained at 100.) Those not elected were allowed to stand, for a constituency in Great Britain, for the House of Commons. All the privileges of the peers of Great Britain were granted to Irish peers, except those elected to the House of Commons—such as Henry Temple, 3rd Viscount Palmerston (1784–1865).

Irish peerages continued to be created during the 19th century, the last being the barony conferred on Lord Curzon before he went to India as viceroy in 1898. New representative peers were chosen from time to time to replace those who had died. No Irish peerage has been created since the proclamation of the Irish Free State in 1922. The last Irish representative peer, the 4th Earl of Kilmorey, died in 1961 (see also p. 71).

It has always been possible for an Irish peer to sit in the House of Lords if he also holds a peerage of Great Britain or the United Kingdom. Thus the Dukes of Leinster and Abercorn, the two highest-ranking Irish peers, are entitled to sit in the Lords as Viscount Leinster and Marquess of Abercorn (both in the peerage of Great Britain), although they are referred to in the House by their higher titles.

The 6th Earl Winterton, an Irish peer, retired from the House of Commons in 1951, after 47 years as a member of Parliament and having held various ministerial posts. In 1952 he was created Baron Turnour in the peerage of the United Kingdom to enable him to sit in the House of Lords.

Great Britain

Peerages of Great Britain were created between 1707 and 1801. During this period peerages of England and Scotland ceased to be created. The 18th century was a period of aristocratic wealth and splendour, and of social mobility, with a peerage the desired consummation of a political career. In 1719 a Bill introduced in the House of Lords designed strictly to limit the number of new peerage creations was defeated in the House of Commons. It was said that the Commons wished to keep the way to the upper House 'as open and as easy as possible'.

Two 'wild acts of anti-Scottish prejudice', in 1709 and 1711, made it impossible for Scottish peers who had also been created peers of Great Britain (for their work in advocating or cementing the Union) to sit in the House of Lords as peers of Great Britain.[23]

United Kingdom

All peerages created after 1801 are peerages of the United Kingdom,[24] with the exception of those Irish peerages created during the 19th century to maintain their total number (see p. 39). From 1801 to 1958 the structure of the House of Lords remained largely unaltered. Until 1911 the Lords had formal legislative parity with the Commons, apart from the matter of taxation, regarded as the preserve of the Commons. Although

[23] In 1709 the Lords laid down that a peer of Great Britain 'might neither vote nor give a proxy in the election of representative peers'. In 1711 they resolved that no Great Britain peerage granted to a Scottish peer entitled him to sit among them.

In 1722 Robert, Marquess of Bowmont, son and heir of the 1st Duke of Roxburghe, was created a peer of Great Britain (Earl Ker) as a reward to his father, who had been Secretary of State. After his majority (from 1730), he sat in the House of Lords, as Earl Ker. In 1741 he succeeded his father as 2nd Duke of Roxburghe, and was excluded from the Lords. Shaw, *The Management of Scottish Society*, p. 10. See also p. 37.

[24] A number of peerages of Great Britain were created after the Act of Union (July 1800), including the earldoms of Cardigan (27 December 1800) and Malmesbury (29 December 1800).

the Life Peerages Act 1958 and the Peerage Act 1963 have affected the structure of the House, no statute has been passed to change its rights and duties, apart from the Parliament Act 1949, which further curtailed its power to delay legislation (see also p. 68).

Hereditary Peers and Peeresses

In the ordinary course a peerage descends to the peer's 'heirs male of his body lawfully begotten', that is, descent is confined to the male line, the peerage passing from father to eldest son or, once it is established in direct descent, to a brother, nephew or male cousin. There are various exceptions, when special arrangements are made at the creation of a peerage for its descent if there is no direct male heir. These arrangements are called remainders. They include the possibility in certain cases of descent to or through females (see also below).

Peeresses in their own Right
Two ancient Scottish earldoms, Mar (cr. c 1115) and Sutherland (cr. c 1235) are at present held by women (the Countess of Mar and the Countess of Sutherland). Ancient baronies by writ may descend to females. Three English baronies serve as examples: that of Willoughby de Eresby (cr. 1313) is held by Baroness Willoughby de Eresby; that of Dacre (cr. 1321) is held by Baroness Dacre; and that of Darcy de Knayth (cr. 1332) is at present held by Baroness Darcy de Knayth.

Various other peerages were created with remainders allowing females to inherit in default of male heirs. Two Scottish earldoms, Loudoun (cr. 1633) and Dysart (cr. 1643), at present exemplify this—the Countess of Loudoun and the Countess of Dysart. So does the English barony of Strange (cr. 1628)—Baroness Strange.

More recent cases are the special remainders in the patents (see p. 47) of distinguished peers who had no son. Thus two British war leaders, the late Earl Mountbatten of Burma (cr. 1947) and the late Viscount Portal of Hungerford (cr. 1946), were succeeded by their elder daughters, the present Countess Mountbatten of Burma and the late Baroness Portal of Hungerford. The former succeeded to all his peerages, the latter to a barony created in 1945.

There have also been examples where a prospective peer has died just before creation and the peerage has been granted to his widow. Thus in 1943 the viscountcy about to be conferred on the former Speaker of the House of Commons, Captain Edward Fitzroy, was granted instead to his wife, who became Viscountess Daventry.

Hereditary peeresses were not entitled to sit in the House of Lords before the passage of the Peerage Act 1963. Of the 16 hereditary peeresses in late 1995, 14 have taken their seats in the House.

Other Remainders

In the peerage of Scotland, there are various remainders, including descent to the senior male heir in a family, even though the direct line from the first peer may be extinct; 'heirs whatsoever' (male or female); or a 'shifting remainder'. An example of the latter is provided by the earldom of Selkirk (cr. 1646), now in the same family as the Dukes of Hamilton (Douglas-Hamilton). When a line of earls has become extinct, the earldom has reverted to the dukedom, and a younger brother of the duke has inherited. In 1994, after the death of the 10th Earl of Selkirk without direct heirs, the earldom reverted. In 1996 the Court of the Lord Lyon ruled that Lord James Douglas-Hamilton, second son of the 14th Duke of Hamilton, was the lawful successor to the peerage. As Lord James, an MP and Minister of State, had disclaimed the title to stay in the House of Commons (see p. 53), his eldest son would eventually succeed.

The exceptionally complicated Letters Patent for the barony of Lucas of Crudwell, bestowed on Mary Lucas in 1663, were designed to prevent it ever falling into abeyance (see p. 49).

In 1708 James Douglas, Duke of Queensberry in Scotland, was created Baron of Rippon and Marquess of Beverly, and Duke of Dover in the peerage of Great Britain, during his natural life,

> with remainder to Charles, Earl of Galloway in Scotland, his second son, and the heirs male of his body, in default of which to George, his third son, and the heirs male of *his* body, with remainders over to other sons successively.

Other remainders have been made, generally to perpetuate the name of someone considered to have given outstanding public service. In 1670 Barbara Palmer (née Villiers; 1641–1709), Countess of Castlemaine, favourite mistress of Charles II ('fairest and lewdest of the royal concubines'), was created Baroness Nonsuch, Countess of Southampton and Duchess of Cleveland, for her noble descent and 'her own personal virtues', with remainder to her first and third natural sons by the King, Charles and George Fitzroy. For Henry St John, Viscount Bolingbroke (and Baron St John of Lydiard Tregoze; cr. 1711) there was a special remainder to his father and his father's other male heirs in case Henry's line should fail. Admiral Viscount Nelson, who had no legitimate children, held three peerages, one of which, the barony of Nelson of the Nile and of Hillborough, was created in 1801 with special remainder to his father and his father's other male issue, and, failing that, to the heirs male of his two sisters. After Nelson's death at Trafalgar in 1805 the barony came to his brother William, who was also created Viscount Merton and Earl Nelson. William was succeeded in 1835 by his nephew Thomas Bolton, who took the surname Nelson, and from whom the present 9th Earl Nelson descends.

There have been a very few cases of succession to a peerage altered by Act of Parliament. Thus Charles, Marquess of Blandford, only surviving son and heir of John Churchill, 1st Duke of Marlborough (cr. 1702), died in 1703, long before his father. An Act in 1706 allowed the elder two of the Duke's four surviving daughters, Henrietta and Anne, and their posterity to succeed to his English peerages. The present 11th Duke is descended from Lady Anne Churchill, wife of Charles Spencer, 3rd Earl of Sunderland.

After 1965 the practice of creating hereditary peers was discontinued. Recently, however, it has been revived, for example in the peerage conferred on a former Prime Minister, Harold Macmillan, who was created Earl of Stockton in 1984, two years before his death.

Life Peerages

The conferment of peerages for life was not unknown in earlier times. Some of these are given overleaf.

—In 1377 Guichard D'Angle, a Poitevin and governor to the young Richard II, was created Earl of Huntingdon for life—he died in 1380.

—In 1385 Richard II's favourite, Robert de Vere, was created Marquess of Dublin for life. In 1386 he surrendered this peerage and was created Duke of Ireland for life instead.

—In 1618 Mary Beaumont, mother of James I's favourite the Duke of Buckingham, was created Countess of Buckingham for life.

—An ambassador from Holland, Jan de Reede, was in 1644 created Baron Reede for life, but with 'no place or voice in Parliament'.

—In 1645 Alice Dudley (d. 1669), deserted wife of Sir Robert Dudley and mother of seven daughters, was created Duchess Dudley for life.

—In 1673 Louise Renée de Penancoët de Kéroualle, who had supplanted the Duchess of Cleveland as favourite mistress of Charles II, was created Duchess of Portsmouth, Countess of Fareham and Baroness Petersfield for life.

—Charles II also created other ladies peeresses for life—for example, in 1674 Anne Bayning a viscountess and Susan Belasyse a baroness; in 1679 Sarah Corbet was created Viscountess Corbet.

—In 1716 Ehrengard Melusina von der Schulenburg (nicknamed 'the Maypole' because of her spare build), senior mistress of George I, was created Duchess of Munster and Marchioness and Countess of Dungannon in the Irish peerage for life. In 1719 she was advanced to Duchess of Kendal, Countess of

Feversham and Baroness Glastonbury for life in the peerage of Great Britain. Their elder daughter, Petronella Melusina (who later married the Earl of Chesterfield), was in 1722 created Countess of Walsingham for life.

—In 1740 the mistress of George II, Amalie Sophie Marianne Wallmoden, was created Countess of Yarmouth for life.

Life Peerages since 1958

Another form of life peerage was created under the Life Peerages Act 1958. This measure was introduced to facilitate the work of the House of Lords by enlarging its field of recruitment and to secure for it the services of outstanding men and women who did not feel able to accept an hereditary title. The peers so created have the rank of baron; they enjoy equal rights and dignities with other peers in all respects except that of passing on the peerage. The Act introduced women to the House of Lords, as life peeresses. The first of the latter to be created were the late Barbara Wootton (Baroness Wootton [of Abinger]) and the late Stella, Dowager Marchioness of Reading (widow of Rufus Isaacs, 1st Marquess of Reading, former Viceroy of India; as Baroness Swanborough). In November 1995 there were 388 life peers, including 65 women.

Life peerages are now the only form of peerage regularly created, either in the half-yearly Honours List (see p. 105) or in special Lists of so-called 'working peers'. These are people nominated by the party leaders, but recommended by the Prime Minister, with the aim of strengthening the ranks of party spokesmen in the House of Lords.

Law Lords

In 1856 the life barony of Wensleydale was conferred on Sir James Parke, a distinguished judge, because of the House of Lords' need for more legal expertise. The validity of this peerage was challenged on the grounds that no life peerage had been granted for 400 years and the power of the Crown to grant such peerages had fallen into disuse. Parke's barony was therefore made hereditary. Under the Appellate Jurisdiction Act 1876 power was taken to appoint a limited number of Lords of Appeal in Ordinary, having the rank of baron and being entitled to sit in the Lords, but not to transmit the dignity to their heirs. They are among the Lords of Appeal, commonly called the Law Lords (the Lord Chancellor, peers who hold or have held high judicial office, and a maximum of 12 Lords of Appeal in Ordinary), of whom at least three must be present at the hearing of an appeal to the House of Lords against the decision of a court of law.

The Creation of Peers

Letters Patent

Since the late 14th century peers have been created by the issue of documents known as Letters Patent. The latter word denotes open and unsealed. Letters Patent have been the traditional means of delivering public directions from the Sovereign under the Great Seal. An intention to grant a peerage is announced in the official *London Gazette* and in the *Edinburgh Gazette*, and after the Letters Patent have been sealed, a second notice is published giving details of the title. For the creation of an hereditary peer Letters Patent use the most formal, and archaic, language. They begin with the Sovereign's full title. They continue:

> Know Ye that We of Our especial grace certain knowledge
> and mere motion do by these Presents advance create and
> prefer Our [followed by the name of the recipient].

They then set out the recipient's rights to the dignity conferred.
The form of words for a life peerage is very formal, but not so
archaic.

Supplementary Peerages

A peer of an older creation will often hold more than one title,
collected by descent and through various remainders over the
years. The Duke of Atholl (cr. 1703) holds 12 other titles—all
in the peerage of Scotland.[25] The Duke of Norfolk holds nine.[26]
The Earl of Portsmouth (cr. 1743) is also Viscount Lymington
and Baron Wallop (both cr. 1720).

The creation of an earl or marquess or royal duke in recent
years has meant the creation of two or three peerages at the same
time. In 1955 the former Prime Minister Clement Attlee was
created Earl Attlee and Viscount Prestwood. In 1984 Harold
Macmillan was created Earl of Stockton and Viscount Macmillan
of Ovenden (see also pp. 44 and 58).

[25] Marquess of Atholl (cr. 1676), Marquess of Tullibardine (cr. 1703), Earl of
Atholl (cr. 1629), Earl of Tullibardine, Earl of Strathtay and Earl of Strathardle
(all cr. 1703), Viscount of Balquhidder (cr. 1676), Viscount Glenalmond and
Viscount Glenlyon (both cr. 1703), Lord Balvenie (cr. 1676), Lord Gask and
Balquhidder (cr. 1606), and Lord Murray of Tullibardine (1604). After the
death of the 10th Duke of Atholl in 1996, his cousin and successor, as 11th
Duke, announced that he would not be using the title.
[26] Earl of Arundel, Earl of Surrey (cr. 1514), Earl of Norfolk (cr. 1644), Baron
Maltravers (cr. 1330), Baron FitzAlan, Baron Clun, Baron Oswaldestre (all cr.
1627), Baron Beaumont (cr. 1309)—all in the peerage of England—and Baron
Howard of Glossop (cr. 1869; peerage of the United Kingdom).

Writs of Summons

The medieval practice of issuing Writs of Summons (see p. 32) has been used in more recent times, though rarely. In 1554, for example, Edward North was summoned to Parliament as Baron North of Kyrteling. Writs of Summons have also been used to accelerate the arrival in the House of Lords of the heir to a peerage—provided that the parent has a lesser peerage. In 1690, for example, Perigrine Osborne, Earl of Danby (a courtesy title—see p. 75), son of Thomas Osborne, Marquess of Carmarthen (and later Duke of Leeds), was summoned to Parliament as Baron Osborne of Kiveton.[27] In 1992 Viscount Cranborne (a courtesy title), eldest son of the 6th Marquess of Salisbury, was summoned to the House of Lords as Lord Cecil.

Abeyance

Abeyance occurs only in the descent of an English peerage, in effect a barony, which is limited in 'fee simple or in tail general'. This applies to old peerages created by Writ of Summons where there is no male heir or no one female heir. Thus if such a peer has two or more daughters, primogeniture does not apply. The peerage, impossible to fragment, cannot be shared between them. It still exists, but is not held by any of the daughters (called co-heirs). Abeyance may come to an end when only one daughter, or the sole heir of one of the daughters, survives. Periods of abeyance may therefore last for many years, even for centuries (see below). The Crown may terminate the abeyance in favour

[27] His father had flown up the steps of the peerage in a successful career. Created Viscount Oseburne in 1673 (see p. 53), then Baron Osborne of Kiveton and Viscount Latimer later in 1673; then Earl of Danby in 1674; then Marquess of Carmarthen in 1689; then Duke of Leeds in 1694. He had also succeeded to his father's baronetcy.

of one of the co-heirs, as happened in 1958 when the barony of de Ros was granted to the elder of two daughters (see p. 59), and the peerage is revived for that person.

Some peerages have been in abeyance since the 15th and 16th centuries. The barony of Dudley (cr. 1439) was in abeyance between 1757 and 1916; those of Strabolgi and Burgh (cr. 1318 and 1529) between 1600 and 1916. The barony of North (see   p. 49) fell into abeyance when the 13th baron was killed in action in 1942. His two sisters are his co-heirs. The barony of Dacre (see p. 41) was called out of abeyance in 1970 in favour of the present Baroness. In 1989 the 5th Lord Grey of Codnor took his seat in the House of Lords, ending an abeyance which had lasted 493 years. His father's claim had begun before the Lords Select Committee in 1926. The barony of Berners went into abeyance in 1992 after the death of the 15th Baroness. In 1995 it was revived in favour of her elder daughter—the 16th Baroness Berners.

A claimant to a peerage in abeyance presents a petition to the Queen through the Home Secretary. If the petition is satis-factory, the Attorney General is asked to provide a report. The petition may be referred to the Committee of Privileges of the House of Lords and the Prime Minister may subsequently rec-ommend to the Queen that the abeyance be terminated. In 1926, a Select Committee on Peerages in Abeyance recommended (special circumstances apart):

— that no abeyance should be terminated, the first commence-ment of which occurred more than one hundred years before the presentation of the petition; and

— that no petition should be allowed to proceed where the petitioner represents less than one-third of the dignity.

Dormant Peerages

A peerage is termed dormant when its holder dies without any obvious heir. There may, however, be doubt that it has actually become extinct, especially if it is an ancient title and legitimate offshoots of the main family stem may have become obscured by time and history.

The earldom of Oxford, in the family of de Vere and dating from 1135, became dormant in 1703, when the 20th Earl, Aubrey de Vere, 'a man of loose morals, but of inoffensive temper and of courtly manners', died leaving one surviving daughter, Lady Diana, who married Charles Beauclerk, 1st Duke of St Albans, son of Charles II and Nell Gwyn. There is still doubt about whether an unknown and unknowing heir exists. Two earldoms of Oxford have been created since 1703, but each has been qualified: the two earldoms, of Oxford and of Mortimer (both now extinct), conferred on the statesman Robert Harley in 1711; and the earldom of Oxford and Asquith, conferred on Herbert Asquith in 1924. The implication is that these styles would differentiate two earldoms of Oxford should a de Vere heir appear.

The Scottish earldom of Annandale and Hartfell (cr. 1662), dormant since 1792, was claimed successfully in 1985 by Patrick Hope Johnstone of Annandale and of that Ilk.

In 1991 the barony of Moynihan became dormant after the death of the 3rd Baron. Succession to the title could not be immediately settled.

Surrender of English Peerages

There have in the past been instances where hereditary peerages have been surrendered to the Crown, though the House of Lords has disputed such decisions. The Lords resolved in 1640 that 'no person that hath any honour in him, and a peer of this realm, may alien or transfer the honour to any other person'. In 1302, for example, the childless Roger Bigod surrendered to Edward I the earldom of Norfolk, his post as earl marshal, and his lands, in return for the lands leased back for life and £1,000 a year. In 1640 the case of Roger Stafford was resolved. He had been brought up in humble circumstances and succeeded to the barony of Stafford at the age of 65 in 1637. He was poor and possessed no lands. Charles I accepted the surrender of the peerage and Roger took £800 in return.

Surrender of Scottish Peerages

Before 1707 it was the law in Scotland that a peer could surrender his peerage or peerages to the King. An example is the earldom of Selkirk (see p. 42), the regulation for the descent of which was changed more than once before the Union.

The surrender of a Scottish peerage could only operate by a deed of resignation in favour of some person or line of heirs specified in the deed, or a person or line to be nominated later by the resigner.

The holder could resign in favour of himself and of a line of heirs different from that laid down in the original grant. He retained the title for his lifetime, but redestined it after his death. This was done to cut out an unsuitable heir, to prevent two peerages being held by one man, or to perpetuate a peerage when an existing line looked like failing.

In the second type of case the holder could resign the title for good. The person specified in the deed would immediately take it up. Seventeenth-century examples include the earldom of

Winton and the viscountcy of Oseburne of Dunblane. The 2nd Earl of Winton, having resigned the title to his younger brother in 1607, became plain 'Robert Seton'. The 1st Viscount Oseburne of Dunblane (cr. 1673) resigned his title to his third son and heir, Perigrine Osborne, in 1674, being described in the deed as 'Thomas *the late* Viscount Osborne of Dunblaine'. The title was then modified to Viscount Dunblane.[28]

Although no resignation, confirmation by the Crown and regrant of a Scottish peerage appear to have happened since the Union of 1707, the Lord Advocate in 1962 gave it as his opinion that the pre-Union procedure had never been abrogated and was still legally competent.

Disclaiming of Peerages

Under the Peerage Act 1963 any hereditary peer of England, Scotland, Great Britain or the United Kingdom may, within one year of inheriting, disclaim his or her peerage for his or her own lifetime. If he or she succeeds to the peerage as a minor, the one-year period takes effect from the 21st birthday. The disclaimer of a peerage is irrevocable. No other hereditary peerage may be conferred on a person who has disclaimed. A life peerage cannot be disclaimed.

As a result of the Peerage Act 1963 a few peerages have been disclaimed. Examples (with dates of disclaimer) include the earldom of Durham (1970); the viscountcies of Hailsham, Stansgate (1963; see p. 69), and Camrose (1995); and the baronies of Altrincham (1963) and Reith (1972).

---

[28] The title was the first step in the peerage of Thomas Osborne (see p. 49).

Degrees of Peerage

There are five degrees in the peerage. These are, in descending order of dignity, dukes, marquesses, earls, viscounts and barons. All life peers are barons and baronesses. The difference in degrees of the peerage is reflected in the formal robes appropriate to each on such occasions as a coronation or the opening of Parliament (see p. 59). All peers but dukes can be described, except in formal documents, by their titles preceded by 'The Lord'; barons are nearly always described thus, rarely as 'Baron'. All peeresses except duchesses can similarly be called 'Lady'.

Dukes

Dukedoms have been comparatively rarely conferred. Before 1623 they were reserved for the King's sons or for men closely allied to the King by family ties. After Queen Elizabeth I had had her kinsman Thomas Howard, 4th Duke of Norfolk, executed for high treason in 1572, there were no dukes in England until James I created George Villiers Duke of Buckingham in 1623. The word comes from *dux*, the Latin for leader. In the present century dukedoms have been conferred only on members of the royal family. The first English dukedom was created in 1337 when Edward the Black Prince, eldest son of Edward III, was created Duke of Cornwall. The first to receive a non-royal dukedom was Thomas Lord Mowbray, created Duke of Norfolk in 1397. He was descended from Thomas of Brotherton, Earl of Norfolk, a younger son of Edward I. In 1726, there were, outside the royal family, some 40 dukes in Great Britain, the highest number ever.

The present Duke of Norfolk is the premier non-royal duke. The title was first granted to the Howard family in 1483, but takes precedence from 1397. The Duke of Norfolk is also premier duke and earl (Earl of Arundel; cr. 1138 or 1292) of England. The premier duke and peer of Scotland is the Duke of Hamilton (cr. 1643). The premier duke of Ireland is the Duke of Leinster (cr. 1766; see p. 76). The last non-royal dukedoms to be conferred were those of Abercorn (cr. 1868) and Westminster (cr. 1874); and, in unusual circumstances, Argyll and Fife.[29]

The wife of a duke is a duchess.

Marquesses

The first instance of a marquessate in England occurred in 1385, when Richard II created Robert de Vere Marquess of Dublin (see p. 45). The word is derived from March, a Teutonic word for a tract of border land; thus again linking peerage with the ownership of land and its implications, including defence. It is also sometimes spelled, incorrectly in England, marquis, because of continental usage. (Marquis is an alternative form in Scotland.) The name was not popular. John Beaufort, Earl of Somerset (eldest son of John of Gaunt) was created Marquess of Dorset in 1397, but compelled to resign the higher dignity just before Richard II's fall in 1399. In 1402 the House of Commons appealed to Henry IV for its restoration. Beaufort asked the King not to restore it: 'the name of Marquess is a strange name in this realm'. In 1532 Anne Boleyn, future wife of Henry VIII, was, with great ceremony, created Marchioness of Pembroke.

[29] George Douglas Campbell (1823–1900), 8th Duke of Argyll in the Scottish peerage, was created Duke of Argyll in the peerage of the United Kingdom in 1892, as a mark of appreciation for his long ministerial career and public service. He had first entered government in 1852, when appointed Lord Privy Seal, and was already KG and KT (see pp. 91 and 93). His eldest son and heir, John, Marquess of Lorne, later 9th Duke, had married Princess Louise, fourth daughter of Queen Victoria, in 1871. For Fife, see p. 73.

She was

> led into his presence by Eleanor countess of Rutland and
> Margaret countess of Sussex. The king invested her with
> the coronet and a crimson velvet mantle furred with
> ermines . . . Henry gave her two patents, one for her
> ennoblement, the other for £1,000 a year 'to maynten hir
> astate'. She thanked him and returned to her chamber.[30]

The only remaining marquess of England is the Marquess of
Winchester (cr. 1551). The premier marquess of Scotland is the
Marquess of Huntly (cr. 1599). The premier marquessate of
Ireland, that of Kildare (cr. 1761), is held by the Duke of
Leinster.

Ten marquessates have been created since 1900. Three[31]
were awarded to former Viceroys of India and one to the first
Governor General of the Commonwealth of Australia.[32] Three—
Cambridge (cr. 1917; extinct), Carisbrooke (cr. 1917; extinct),
and Milford Haven (cr. 1917)—were granted to members of the
Teck and Mountbatten families who had given up their German
princely titles.[33]

The wife of a marquess is styled marchioness.

Earls

Earldoms are of greater antiquity and the term was in use before
the Norman Conquest in 1066. It is connected with 'jarl', the

---

[30] Miller, *Henry VIII and the English Peerage*, p. 24.
[31] Curzon of Kedelston (cr. 1921; extinct), Reading (cr. 1926) and Willingdon
(cr. 1936; extinct).
[32] Linlithgow (cr. 1902).
[33] The other three 20th-century marquessates are Aberdeen (cr. 1916), Crewe
(cr. 1911; extinct) and Lincolnshire (see p. 15).

old Norse word for chieftain. In pre-Conquest days an earl was ruler, under the King, of large areas of England, such as Northumberland, Mercia or Wessex.

Under the Norman Kings the government of an earl was normally restricted to one county and became hereditary. Sometime between 1135 and 1141 both King Stephen and his rival for the throne, Matilda (daughter of Henry I), created Geoffrey de Mandeville Earl of Essex with inheritance to his heirs. Other powerful earls were the Bigods, earls of Norfolk, the de Burghs, earls of Kent, and the de Clintons, earls of Huntingdon. In 1328 Roger Mortimer was created Earl of March—not a territorial designation—and the dignity is said thereby to have lost some of its significance. Nevertheless the Percy earls of Northumberland (cr. 1342) and the Nevill earls of Westmorland (cr. 1364), for example, were magnates in northern England until their male lines died out in 1668 and 1601 respectively.

In the English peerage the oldest earldoms still extant are those of Arundel (see p. 55), Shrewsbury (cr. 1442), Derby (cr. 1485), Huntingdon (cr. 1529) and Pembroke (cr. 1551). Old Scottish earldoms still extant are Mar, Crawford (cr. 1398), Erroll (whose holder is hereditary Lord High Constable of Scotland; cr. 1452), Caithness (cr. 1455), Rothes (cr. c 1457), Morton (cr. 1458) and Buchan (cr. 1469). The 1st Earl of Shrewsbury (John Talbot) was created Earl of Waterford in the peerage of Ireland in 1446.

From the 17th century the territorial designation of an earldom, which had become more a title of honour than a sign of local power, has not necessarily meant that its holder is the main landowner or temporal authority in the area (or city, or town) designated.

The premier earldom of Scotland is that of Mar (see p. 37). The Earl of Crawford and Balcarres is the premier earl on the

Union Roll of Scotland. The premier earldom of Ireland is that of Kildare (cr. 1316), held by the Duke of Leinster.

As titles of honour, earldoms have been awarded in later centuries to men prominent in public life and to reward outstanding public service. An earldom has also been awarded to retired prime ministers: Stanley Baldwin, created Earl Baldwin of Bewdley in 1937, and Clement Attlee, created Earl Attlee in 1955, are two 20th-century examples.

The wife of an earl is styled countess.

Viscounts

Viscountcies date from 1440, when King Henry VI (who was also crowned King of France) created John Lord Beaumont, Viscount Beaumont in England. In 1441 he created him Viscount Beaumont in France—a step towards integrating the titles of the two countries. Like the title of marquess (see p. 55) it did not take on. Few viscounts were created until the 17th century.

The word derives from vice, meaning deputy or assistant, and count.

The tradition of awarding a viscountcy to retired Speakers of the House of Commons was revived in 1983 when Mr George Thomas was created Viscount Tonypandy. The premier viscount of England is Viscount Hereford (cr. 1550). The premier viscount of Scotland is Viscount Falkland (cr. 1620). The premier viscount of Ireland is Viscount Gormanston (cr. 1478).

The wife of a viscount is styled viscountess.

Barons

A barony in modern times is the lowest degree in the peerage. In medieval times in England it evolved into an hereditary dignity conferred by the Crown. In Scotland the equivalent of a baron is a Lord of Parliament.

The first barony created by Letters Patent—the first peerage conferred as a purely personal honour—was in 1387, when Richard II created John Beauchamp de Holt, Baron of Kyderminster, with remainder to his male heirs. Baronies by Writ of Summons, however, continued to be created after this date.

The premier barony of England is that of de Ros (cr. 1264; see p. 50), held by Lord de Ros. The premier baron of England is Lord Mowbray, Segrave and Stourton, the titles dating from 1283, 1295 and 1448 respectively. The premier lord of Scotland is Lord Forbes (cr. 1445), and the premier baron of Ireland is Lord Kingsale (cr. 1397).

The wife of a baron is styled baroness.

Robes of Peers and Peeresses

The full robes of peers and peeresses are now worn only at coronations. The coronets (illustrated between pp. 00 and 00) are worn above a cap of maintenance[34]—crimson velvet, turned up ermine, with a golden tassel on top. The coronets of barons, viscounts, earls and marquesses—and their female equivalents—have a circle of silver gilt as their base. On a baron's coronet the circle is surmounted by six silver balls; on a viscount's it is surmounted by 16 silver balls; on an earl's by eight silver balls raised on points, with gold strawberry leaves between the points; on a marquess's by four gold strawberry leaves and four silver balls, placed alternately, the latter somewhat raised on points

---

[34] A cap or hat worn as a symbol of official dignity.

above the rim. A duke's coronet is a circle of gold surmounted by eight golden strawberry leaves.

Peeresses' coronets, smaller than those for male peers, may be placed inside a tiara.

All robes are mantles of crimson velvet edged with miniver (plain white fur); the cape is pure miniver. For a baron the cape is ornamented with two rows of spots of ermine; for a viscount with two and a half rows of spots of ermine; for an earl with three rows; for a marquess with three and a half rows; and for a duke with four rows. The mantles of peeresses are edged with pure miniver, of varying breadth (from 2 inches for a baroness to 5 inches for a duchess), and have trains (from 3 feet for a baroness to 6 feet for a duchess).

At the coronation of George III in 1761, wrote Horace Walpole, 'My Lady Harrington, covered with all the diamonds she could borrow, hire, or seize, and with the air of Roxana, was the finest figure at a distance.'[35] Another observer wrote: 'The ladies made a glorious appearance. Wherever there was any beauty of countenance, or shape, or air, they were all heightened by the dress.'[36]

For his ceremonial introduction into the House of Lords a newly created peer will wear scarlet parliamentary robes and carry a black cocked hat. A peeress wears identical robes and also wears a tricorn hat throughout the ceremony.

---

[35] *Letters* (1857–59), III, 437–8.
[36] *Mrs [Elizabeth] Montagu's Letters* (1813), iv, 364.

The Peerage: Titles and Privileges

Prefixes

In strict usage the formal prefixes for peers are as follows:

Duke/Duchess	The Most Noble the; or His/Her Grace the
Marquess/Marchioness	The Most Honourable the
Earl/Countess	The Right Honourable the
Viscount/Viscountess	The Right Honourable the
Baron/Baroness	The Right Honourable the

In ordinary correspondence 'The' is sufficient prefix to the titles cited above.

Forms of Address and Styles

All peers above the rank of baron are formally addressed as 'cousin' by the Sovereign. The ancient and formal greeting from the Sovereign to a duke is 'Right trusty and right entirely beloved cousin'; to an earl 'Right trusty and well beloved cousin'; to a baron 'Right trusty and well beloved'.

In correspondence or in conversation the term 'Your Grace' is seldom used. 'Duke', 'Duchess', 'Lord Framville', 'Lady Blencarn' are used in conversation rather than the formal 'Your Grace' or 'My Lord' or 'Your Ladyship', which nowadays could be taken to imply a hint of subservience.

A duke or duchess is always referred to as 'The Duke of Bonchester' or 'The Duchess of Bonchester'. Other peers and peeresses are generally referred to in everyday usage as 'Lord' or 'Lady'. Thus the Marquess of Fulbeck would be styled Marquess of Fulbeck in formal documents and on first mention in speech or writing. Thereafter he is normally referred to as 'Lord Fulbeck'. The same would apply to Viscountess Liverton, who would, in similar cases, be referred to as 'Lady Liverton'. Barons and baronesses, however, except in formal documents, are always referred to as 'Lord Blencarn' or 'Lady Blencarn', never as 'Baron Blencarn' or 'Baroness Blencarn'. There are two exceptions. English peeresses in their own right are often referred to as Baroness, to emphasise the fact that they hold the distinction in their own right. Life baronesses under the Life Peerages Act 1958 are also referred to as Baroness. Scottish ladies, such as Lady Saltoun (cr. 1445) or Lady Herries of Terregles (cr. 1490), are never referred to as Baroness (see p. 37).

A forename must never be placed between a title and a peerage name. It is therefore incorrect, on any occasion, to address or refer to a peer or peeress as Lord John Fulbeck, Viscountess Caroline Liverton, or Lady Mary Blencarn.

The husband of a peeress in her own right or of a life peeress derives no title or status from his wife.

Titles of Peers and Peeresses

The traditional association between peerage and landownership continues to be reflected in the way placenames are often used in the titles of peers, although they may not necessarily own land. The tendency in recent years has been for the surname to be used for the titles of viscounts and barons, and sometimes for earls.

All ducal styles are followed by the word 'of': for example, the Duke of Wellington. The titles of all marquesses and earls are generally followed by the word 'of': the Marquess of Winchester, the Earl of Dundee. There are, however, some exceptions. Four existing marquessates do not take the prefix: Camden (cr. 1812), Conyngham (cr. 1816), Douro (cr. 1814; held by the Duke of Wellington) and Townshend (cr. 1787). Nor do between 30 and 40 earldoms, for example: Cadogan (cr. 1800), Ferrers (cr. 1711), Jellicoe (cr. 1925), Peel (1929), Sondes (cr. 1880) and Waldegrave (cr. 1729). Three 20th-century earldoms where the surname is used before the 'of' have been conferred by special permission on two former Prime Ministers—Baldwin of Bewdley (cr. 1937) and Lloyd George of Dwyfor (cr. 1945)—and a distinguished war leader and former Viceroy of India—Mountbatten of Burma (cr. 1947).

The word 'of' never appears in the everyday usage of the titles of viscounts or barons, except in a few cases in the Scottish peerage (for example, Viscount of Oxfuird [cr. 1651]; Viscount of Arbuthnott [cr. 1641]). For viscounts and barons, however, a territorial designation is essential when the Letters Patent are made out. Thus, having chosen his title, Viscount Liverton would be gazetted as Viscount Liverton, of Easton in the county of Suffolk; Lord Blencarn as Baron Blencarn, of Warminster in the county of Wiltshire. Nevertheless, they would always be known as Viscount (or Lord) Liverton and Lord Blencarn—never as Lord Liverton of Easton or Lord Blencarn of Warminster.

A territorial designation, however, is sometimes appended to a title, especially when the surname is used, to distinguish one peerage from another of the same name. In such a case there is a double territorial designation. The peerage of Viscount Montgomery of Alamein (cr. 1946) is distinguished from the earldom of Montgomery (cr. 1605; held by the Earl of Pembroke) and the Scottish lordship of Montgomerie (cr. 1449; held by the Earl of Eglinton and Winton). In full, the title is Viscount Montgomery of Alamein, of Hindhead in the county of Surrey. The life peerage conferred on the former cabinet minister Norman St John-Stevas in 1987 was that of St John of Fawsley. There was already a barony of St John of Bletso (cr. 1559) and a viscountcy of Bolingbroke and St John (cr. 1712). Three old titles, the barony of Vaux of Harrowden (cr. 1523) and the Scottish lordships of Saltoun of Abernethy (see p. 62) and Herries of Terregles were so created.

Occasionally a new peer has adopted his hyphenated forename and surname as a title: for example the politician Lord Noel-Buxton (cr. 1930), and Lord George-Brown (cr. 1970), a life peer and former Foreign and Commonwealth Secretary. Field Marshal Sir Alan Brooke, another distinguished war leader, fused his forename and surname when created Viscount Alanbrooke in 1946.

Scotsmen and women who are created peers may not take their surname alone as a peerage title unless they are Chief of their Name or Clan.[37]

[37] New rules on this question were introduced in 1965. Where a Scotsman or woman belongs to an 'organised' family (for which chiefly arms have been recorded in the *Public Register of All Arms and Bearings in Scotland*) the surname alone may not be taken as a peerage title. Where the holder of a surname, who is not the chief and is not to be recognised as the chief, is elevated to the peerage, the title given to him, if he wishes to use his surname, is the surname with a territorial designation. Thus, for example, Lord Cameron of Lochbroom or Lord Campbell of Croy. Where the family is not organised, then the name may be taken alone—for example, Lord McCluskey or Lord Sewel.

Titles have, very occasionally, been duplicated. For example, there is an earldom of Arran in the Scottish peerage (cr. 1643; held by the Duke of Hamilton) and another in the Irish peerage (cr. 1762). One of the titles of Prince Charles is Earl of Carrick in the Scottish peerage (cr. c 1186). There is also an earldom of Carrick in the Irish peerage (cr. 1762). The Duke of Buccleuch also holds the dukedom of Queensberry (cr. 1684) in the Scottish peerage. This is to be distinguished from the title of the Marquess of Queensberry (cr. 1682), also in the Scottish peerage.

An overseas territorial designation has been adopted, exceptionally in the case of civilians, where the recipient of a peerage has strong connections with a certain place. An example, apart from Earl Mountbatten of Burma and Lord Montgomery of Alamein (see pp. 63–4), is the life peerage conferred on Sue Ryder (founder of the Sue Ryder homes) in 1979: Baroness Ryder of Warsaw. Two first world war leaders, Field Marshals Sir John French and Sir Herbert Kitchener, became respectively Earl of Ypres and Earl Kitchener of Khartoum.

Garter King of Arms has to approve a new peer's choice of title, in accordance with certain rules. Lord Lyon King of Arms is consulted when a Scottish element is desired in the title.

A peer signs himself by his title, without a prefix or forename. Thus the signature of the Earl of Longford, publisher and politician, is simply 'Longford'; that of Lord St John of Fawsley is 'St John of Fawsley'.

A peeress in her own right or a life peeress signs herself with her title only. Lady Sutherland (see p. 41) signs 'Sutherland'; Baroness Ryder of Warsaw 'Ryder of Warsaw'. A peeress by marriage—the wife of a peer—places her forename in front of her title. Thus the Duchess of Devonshire signs 'Deborah Devonshire'.

Widows of Peers

The widow of a peer is 'the Dowager'. So the widow of the Earl of Framville is 'The Dowager Countess of Framville'. If a new peer is unmarried, it is not unknown for the widowed peeress (generally his mother) to continue to call herself 'The Countess of Framville', not strictly speaking correctly, until he does marry and his wife becomes Countess of Framville. Most widowed peeresses nowadays prefer to put their forenames before their titles—for example, Charlotte Countess of Framville—to distinguish them from their successors.

Should a peer's widow remarry, she takes the title of her new husband, and, if the new husband is not a peer, she ceases to be a peeress. Some former peeresses continue to call themselves by their former titles and history has various examples of this practice. Although not unlawful, the continued use of the title is 'merely a matter of courtesy and allowed by the usages of society'.

Divorced Peeresses

If a peer and peeress are divorced, the wife ceases to be a peeress, although it is accepted that she may continue to use the title if she does not remarry. In such a case the title is regarded as a name only, and not denoting the rank and status of a peeress. If the husband remarries, his new wife becomes the peeress and the former wife puts her forename before the title. Thus the former wife of the remarried Marquess of Fulbeck may call herself Anne Marchioness of Fulbeck—to distinguish her from the new Marchioness of Fulbeck. If she remarries, she adopts the title of her new husband.

The position in Scotland is different. A divorced peeress is regarded as a widow, and therefore, by implication, is still a peeress until she remarries.[38] Thus the former wife of the remarried Duke of Drumour would be Joan Duchess of Drumour. Even should she remarry, she may continue, under Scottish custom, to call herself Joan Duchess of Drumour—as an alias.

Privileges of Peers

There are few privileges still enjoyed by peers and not by commoners. Peers are exempt from jury service and they may not be arrested in the course of a civil action. But their most significant privilege is their actual or potential membership of the House of Lords, the upper chamber of Parliament (and the supreme court of appeal in criminal cases in England, Wales and Northern Ireland, and in civil cases throughout Britain, although only Law Lords participate when it is performing its judicial functions).

Until 1911 the House of Lords had formal legislative parity with the Commons, although for several centuries taxation had come to be regarded as the preserve of the Commons. The rejection by the Lords of the Liberal Government's budget of 1909 led to a crisis which ended in legislation defining the relations between the two Houses and limiting the powers of the

[38] In 1887 the Marchioness of Queensberry (Sibyl Montgomery) divorced her husband, John Sholto Douglas, 9th Marquess of Queensberry, originator of the Queensberry rules and enemy of Oscar Wilde. He died in 1900 and was succeeded by his eldest surviving son and his wife, the 10th Marquess and Marchioness of Queensberry. In 1902 Sibyl Marchioness of Queensberry received no summons to the coronation of Edward VII. She claimed her right to attend as a peeress, but the Lord Chancellor, the Earl of Halsbury, refused her claim. Her case was then heard before the Scottish Law Officers. The Scottish Lord Advocate, Sir Andrew Murray, considered that the Lord Chancellor had been wrong. Lady Queensberry was duly summoned to the coronation.

Lords to delay a Bill—for two years only. In 1949 the Parliament Act further curtailed its power to delay legislation. The Criminal Justice Act 1948 abolished the right of a peer to be tried 'before his peers'.

Cases of trial by peers include that of Laurence Shirley, 4th Earl Ferrers in 1760, tried by his fellow peers sitting in Westminster Hall, convicted and hanged at Tyburn for the murder of his land steward.[39] In 1776 Elizabeth Chudleigh (1720–88), supposed widow of Evelyn Pierrepont, 2nd Duke of Kingston, whom she had married in 1769, was tried for bigamy before the House of Lords, sitting in Westminster Hall, and found guilty. Her reputation went before her—a beautiful woman but 'remarkable for the freedom and indelicacy of her conduct'.[40] She could have been burned on the hand, but she claimed 'privilege of her peerage'. Augustus John Hervey, the man whom the Lords decided she was legally married to (from 1744), had meanwhile become 3rd Earl of Bristol; and so she remained a peeress. In 1901, John, 2nd Earl Russell was also tried for bigamy. George V granted him a free pardon in 1911. The last occasion was the trial in 1935 of the 26th Lord de Clifford on a charge of manslaughter following a road accident. Eighty-four peers were present and Lord de Clifford was found not guilty.

[39] Lord Ferrers was 'the first sufferer by the new drop just then introduced in the place of the barbarous cart, ladder and medieval three-cornered gibbet'.

[40] She appeared in 1749 at a masked ball in the character of Iphigenia, 'so naked that you would have taken her for Andromeda' (Horace Walpole, *Letters*, II, 153). At Berlin in 1765 King Frederick II of Prussia related how she 'emptied two bottles of wine and staggered as she danced, and nearly fell on the floor'. In 1777 she visited Russia, where she was made much of and was on good terms with Catherine II. A contemporary couplet went:

A Maid like me Heaven form'd at least for two.
I married him—and now I'll marry you.

(Walpole, *Letters*, VII, 297).

Membership of Parliament

At present most peers over the age of 21 are entitled to sit in the House of Lords. Royal dukes may claim their place in the House but do not normally attend. The Prince of Wales, however, has attended and has spoken on more than one occasion. Peers of Ireland (see p. 38) who do not hold a peerage of England, Scotland, Great Britain or the United Kingdom, are not entitled to sit in the House of Lords. They may, however, sit on the steps of the throne and listen to debates from there. They may also, if they wish, stand as candidates for the House of Commons. An example is Mr Richard Needham, the Conservative Member of Parliament for Chippenham and former Minister of State. He is the 6th Earl of Kilmorey and does not use his title, though there is no constitutional objection to his doing so. Peers of Ireland may also vote in elections in constituencies for which they have a residential qualification.

Because of the link between membership of the peerage and membership of the House of Lords, peers (apart from peers of Ireland) are debarred from voting in the election for members of the House of Commons or offering themselves as candidates. Those peers who have disclaimed (see p. 53), however, are entitled to seek election to the House of Commons.

Among cases of disclaiming was that of Mr Anthony Wedgwood Benn (Tony Benn), a member of the House of Commons, who in 1960 succeeded his father as 2nd Viscount Stansgate—against his will. His petition to the House of Lords to be allowed to renounce the title was unsuccessful. He stood as a candidate in the ensuing by-election for his seat and won, but was not allowed back into the Commons. He campaigned for a change in the law, which took place with the Peerage Act 1963. As soon as the Act became law he renounced his title, stood again for his old constituency and was returned to the House of Commons.

Bearers of courtesy titles (see p. 75) may sit in the House of Commons.

At November 1995 there were 1159 peers (excluding dormant, abeyant and 11 disclaimed titles), of whom four were peers of the blood royal, five were minors and 388 were life peers. These figures also include eight hereditary English peeresses, seven hereditary Scottish peeresses, one hereditary United Kingdom peeress and 65 life peeresses. In addition, there were 69 Irish peers (19 earls, 15 viscounts and 35 barons) who did not hold any other peerage which would enable them to sit in the House of Lords.

Some peers (about 80 in late 1995) who do not wish to participate in the proceedings of the House of Lords, do not go through the necessary formalities on inheriting their title. They therefore do not receive Writs of Summons to Parliament. Others receive a Writ, but obtain leave of absence. Average daily attendance in the House of Lords (including hereditary and life peers) is 376.

The Peerage: Other Topics

The Irish Peerage and the House of Lords

In 1966 the 8th Earl of Antrim and other Irish peers petitioned the House of Lords to ask that elections of Irish representative peers (see p. 38) should again be held. The Committee of Privileges concluded that the Irish Free State Agreement Act 1922 had dismantled this electoral structure and that no more elections could be made without further legislation.

In 1995 the 12th Lord Farnham, another Irish peer, petitioned for the right to sit in the Lords. His grandfather, the 11th baron (d. 1957), had been one of the last surviving Irish representative peers. In Lord Farnham's view, the issuing of Writs of Summons to the surviving representative peers after the 1922 legislation meant that a barony had been created by writ in the person of his grandfather, to which he was the rightful heir.

The Committee concluded that the 11th Lord Farnham had been elected to the House for life and that no barony by writ could have been created. One of the Lords of Appeal said: 'It is absolutely clear that no question of a Barony by Writ arises here, even if there were a competence, these days, to create it'.

Hereditary Peerages Bill and Re-creation of Peerages

Recent cases have pointed to the impossibility of amending Letters Patent to change the line of succession to a peerage. In

1992 Lord Diamond, a life peer, introduced a Bill into the House of Lords to provide

> an option for all those hereditary Peers who do not wish to continue the present practice under which, on their death, an elder daughter will be wholly disregarded in favour of a younger son.

Under it, the Crown would be given powers to amend the Letters Patent, so that in future the peerage would pass to the eldest child, whether male or female.

Opposition to the Bill focused on the unfairness of depriving existing heirs male of something that they had always had a right to expect. The Lord Chancellor raised three points:

—whether it was right to alter Letters Patent granted long ago and even to cause dissension within families by diverting descent of a peerage;

—the problems for those peerages where arrangements had been made for property to descend to male heirs and where property would become separated from the title; and

—the undesirability of involving the Queen in family disputes when the Crown might have to decide between the claims of an existing heir and an eldest daughter.

The Bill was defeated.

In 1994 Lord Diamond tried again, with an amended Bill, providing that 'on the death of the present holder of the title the Letters Patent will be amended so as to provide, with certain exceptions, for the eldest child or other relative to succeed, whether male or female'. The power of a present holder of a peerage to choose who should succeed to it had been removed. Again, the Lords rejected the Bill.

In 1889, after his marriage to Princess Louise, eldest daughter of the Prince of Wales (later Edward VII), the 6th Earl of Fife (Alexander William George Duff) was created Duke of Fife and Marquess of Macduff with remainder to his heirs male. In 1900, having had no son, he was again created Duke of Fife (and Earl of Macduff), with a special remainder to his two daughters and their male issue. He was succeeded by his elder daughter, Princess Alexandra (who married her cousin Prince Arthur of Connaught), who was in turn succeeded by the present 3rd Duke of Fife, son of the 1st Duke's younger daughter, Princess Maud (Countess of Southesk, wife of Charles Alexander Carnegie, 11th Earl of Southesk).

In 1756 the First Lord of the Treasury, Thomas Pelham-Holles, 1st Duke of Newcastle, without male heirs, wanted his nephew Henry Fynes, 9th Earl of Lincoln, to succeed him. He prevailed on George II to create him Duke of Newcastle-under-Lyme, with a special remainder so that his nephew could succeed. The old dukedom (of Newcastle-upon-Tyne) became extinct at his death in 1768, and Lord Lincoln duly succeeded to the new dukedom of Newcastle.

Suspended Peerages

The Titles Deprivation Act 1917 deprived of their peerages peers and princes who had been enemies of Britain during the First World War. It did not extinguish the peerage, as an Act of forfeiture under attainder had done. It suspended the rights of then holders, and of other persons named, 'to enjoy and possess the peerage' until an application could be made by an heir for the peerage's restitution.

Those deprived of their peerages were Prince Ernst, Duke of Brunswick and Lüneburg, and also 3rd Duke of Cumberland and Teviotdale (and Earl of Armagh) in the peerage of Great Britain (descended from George III); and Heinrich, Count Taaffe in the Austrian nobility (12th Viscount Taaffe, and Baron of Ballymote, in the peerage of Ireland). Deprived of his peerage, and his dignity of Royal Highness, was Prince Leopold Charles, 2nd Duke of Albany (and Earl of Clarence and Baron Arklow), son of Prince Leopold, 1st Duke of Albany (see pp. 103 and 139).

No petition has been presented to the Crown in respect of the restitution of any of these peerages.

Katherine Parr, Queen of England
(1512–48; Queen Regent 1544;
Queen Dowager 1547–48).

Queen Mary I and King Philip,
from the Hilary Plea Roll of 1558.

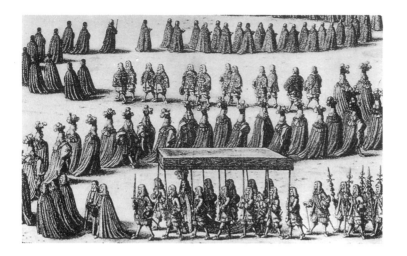

Garter Procession at Windsor (early 1670s) showing King Charles II under the canopy. In front of him walk the officers of the Order, the Knights Companions and the officers of arms.

Coronation of King James II and Queen Mary Beatrice at Westminster Abbey in 1685. Francis Sandford's detailed account of this coronation shows the first use of what have become the standardised styles of coronation robes and coronets for peers and peeresses.

A contemporary view of the Duchess of Kingston entering Westminster Hall for her trial in 1776: 'attended by her Chaplain, Physician, Apothecary, and three Maids of Honor'.

An Earl.

A Marquis.

'wo peers in parliamentary robes (with coronets also illustrated; c 1824).

Installation of Howe Peter Browne, 2nd Marquess of Sligo, as a Knight of St Patrick in St Patrick's Cathedral, Dublin, in 1819. Painting by Joseph Peacock. It also shows, among others, the Lord Lieutenant of Ireland (and Grand Master of the Order), Earl Talbot, and his wife (under canopies); many Irish peers and peeresses; and Ulster King of Arms.

The House of Lords in London debating Home Rule for Ireland in September 1893.

Sir Cliff Richard, after receiving his knighthood in 1995.

PC John Healy after his investiture with the Queen's Gallantry Medal in 1991.

The Queen, The Duke of Edinburgh and Prince Charles Duke of Rothesay at Holyroodhouse in Edinburgh before a ceremony of the Order of the Thistle in 1991.

The Lord Lyon King of Arms and the Scottish officers of arms in front of Holyrood Abbey in 1991. *From left*: Kintyre Pursuivant, Rothesay Herald, the Lord Lyon (Sir Malcolm Innes of Edingight), Ross Herald, and Unicorn Pursuivant.

Insignia

Badge of a CBE.

Badge of an LVO.

From top left: Lesser George, Star, and Garter—once belonging to Robert Banks Jenkinson, 2nd Earl of Liverpool, Prime Minister 1812–27.

Insignia: Collar, Star and Badge of a Knight Grand
Cross of the Order of St Michael and St George.

The Victoria Cross
awarded to Sjt. J. Clarke
of the Lancashire Fusiliers.

Insignia

Badge of the Order of Merit.

Badge of a Companion of Honour.

Badge of a Baronet

Badge of a Knight Bachelor

Coronation of Queen Elizabeth II in 1953. The ceremony of recognition. *In front and from left*: the Archbishop of Canterbury (Dr Geoffrey Fisher); the Lord High Chancellor (Lord Simonds); the Lord Great Chamberlain (5th Marquess of Cholmondeley); the Lord High Constable of England (Viscount Alanbrooke); the Earl Marshal of England (16th Duke of Norfolk). *To left*: peeresses, officers of arms, and bishops.

The Coronation of Queen Elizabeth II in 1953.
The Duke of Norfolk pays homage.

The Queen and the Duke of Edinburgh, Queen Elizabeth The Queen Mother, and President Hosni Mubarak of Egypt and Mrs Mubarak before a State banquet at Buckingham Palace in 1991. The Queen Mother and the Duke of Edinburgh wear the insignia of the Garter. The Queen Mother also wears the family orders of King George VI and Queen Elizabeth II. Around his neck the Duke also wears the Order of Merit. President Mubarak wears the Star of a Knight Grand Cross of the Order of the Bath. The Queen wears the collar of the Egyptian Order of the Nile and the family orders of King George V and King George VI.

Courtesy Titles

Sons and Heirs to Peerages

The eldest, or only, sons and heirs of hereditary peers are not peers during the lifetime of the holder of the peerage unless they themselves are made peers in their own right (see p. 49). It is usual, however, to refer to them by 'courtesy' titles. If the holder of the peerage has other peerages as well, these provide courtesy titles for the heir. For example, the son and heir of the Duke of Devonshire (cr. 1694) is known as Marquess of Hartington, a lesser peerage of his father; the eldest son of the Marquess of Salisbury (cr. 1789) as Viscount Cranborne; and the son and heir of the Earl of Snowdon (cr. 1961) as Viscount Linley.

The peerage need not be the next senior peerage held by the father. For example, the Duke of Manchester's next senior peerage is the earldom of Manchester (see p. 36). For obvious reasons his son and heir is known by the *next* senior peerage held by the father—Viscount Mandeville. Three earls—for various historical reasons—hold no other peerage. Custom has invented a courtesy title for the son and heir of each: Viscount Hastings for the son and heir of the Earl of Huntingdon; Lord Courtenay for the son and heir of the Earl of Devon; Lord Langton for the son and heir of Earl Temple of Stowe (cr. 1822). There is also a case of an invented courtesy title where the peer does have other titles: should an Earl of Enniskillen (cr. 1789), who is also Viscount Enniskillen and Baron Mountflorence, all in the peerage of Ireland, and Baron Grinstead (cr. 1815) in the peerage of the United Kingdom, have a son and heir, he would, by custom, be called Viscount Cole.

The system in full use can go into four generations. Thus during the lifetime of the late 7th Duke of Leinster (d. 1976), his son and heir was Marquess of Kildare; *his* elder son and heir was Earl of Offaly; and *his* infant son and heir was Viscount Leinster.

A peerage used as a courtesy title does not take the prefix 'the'. The designation is 'Marquess of Blandford' or 'Lord Blandford', not 'the' Marquess of Blandford or 'the' Lord Blandford.

Younger Children

Younger sons of dukes and marquesses take the title 'Lord' before their forename and surname. Thus the eldest son and heir of the Duke of Bonchester (family name Ormont) is Marquess of Bedfont. His younger sons are Lord Richard Ormont, Lord David Ormont and Lord James Ormont. The daughters of dukes, marquesses and earls take the title 'Lady' before their forename and surname. The daughter of the Duke of Bonchester is Lady Rose Ormont. It is incorrect, on any occasion, to refer to them as Lord Ormont or Lady Ormont.

The wife of Lord Richard Ormont would be Lady Richard Ormont (addressed always as 'Lady Richard'). If Lady Rose Ormont marries, she takes her husband's surname, unless he is a peer, in which case she takes his style. Thus if she marries Mr Archie Robinson, she becomes Lady Rose Robinson. If she marries Lord Blencarn, she becomes Lady Blencarn. If she marries Lord Julian Smythe, younger son of the Marquess of Fulbeck, she will be Lady Rose Smythe, unless she chooses to be known as Lady Julian Smythe—the daughter of a duke ranking above the younger son of a marquess. If she marries Viscount FitzHenry, son and heir of the Earl of Framville, she may, if she wishes, call herself Lady Rose FitzHenry (in preference to Viscountess FitzHenry), a duke's daughter taking precedence over the elder son of an earl.

The younger sons of earls and the sons and daughters of viscounts and barons are styled Honourable (abbreviated to Hon.). Thus a younger son of the Earl of Framville (family name FitzHenry) would be the Hon. Edward FitzHenry, while his sister would be Lady Violet FitzHenry. The daughter and son of Viscount Liverton (family name Butler) would be the Hon. Jane Butler and the Hon. Piers Butler. If the Hon. Jane marries a Mr George Brown, she becomes the Hon. Mrs Brown. If the Hon. Piers Butler marries Miss Pamela Jones, Miss Jones becomes the Hon. Mrs Piers Butler. In everyday usage Lord Richard and Lady Rose are addressed as 'Lord Richard' and 'Lady Rose'. The Hon. Jane, the Hon. Piers and the Hon. Mrs Piers are addressed as 'Miss Butler', 'Mr Butler' and 'Mrs Butler'.

Children of life peers or life peeresses are also styled Honourable, like the children of hereditary barons and baronesses.

Children of Holders of Courtesy Peerages

The eldest sons of holders of courtesy peerages generally assume their grandfather's next senior title and are called second heirs. Thus the eldest son of the Marquess of Bedfont is Earl of Hallington; Lord Bedfont's younger children would be styled as the sons and daughters of a marquess: Lord Antony Ormont and Lord Simon Ormont; Lady Verity Ormont. Lord FitzHenry's children would be styled the same as the children of a viscount;

and so on. The children of younger children of peers and holders of courtesy titles have no title.

Scottish Titles

The heirs apparent or presumptive to peers in Scotland may hold the dignity of 'The Master' of whatever is the peerage title. Thus the eldest son of Lord Elphinstone (cr. 1509) is the Master of Elphinstone. The son of Lord Aberdour, heir apparent of the Earl of Morton, is Master of Aberdour. (No 'the'; he is second heir apparent.)

In the case of the eldest son and heir apparent 'Master' is a substantive dignity and not a courtesy title. In the case of a grandson it is a courtesy title. The eldest sons and heirs of Scottish dukes, marquesses and earls are nowadays known so-cially by one of their fathers' other peerages, but the title Master, strictly speaking, applies to all eldest sons of Scottish peers, whatever their rank—even though they may not use it socially. They were also once entitled to sit in the Scottish Parliament, but not to speak or vote. Thus the son and heir of the Marquess of Huntly, socially Earl of Aboyne, is *legally* The Master of Huntly.

The wife of a Master is not called 'Mistress of', but 'The Hon. Mrs', prefixed to the family surname. The heiress pre-sumptive to a title would be 'The Mistress' (not often used).

Widows and Divorced Wives

The widow of a holder of a peerage used as a courtesy title still uses the title, with her forename in front of it if necessary (Abigail Countess of Hallington), until she remarries, as in the case of peeresses (see p. 66). The widow of Lord Richard Ormont or the Hon. Piers Butler continues to call herself Lady Richard Ormont or the Hon. Mrs Piers Butler until remarriage.

In the case of divorce the same applies as in the case of peeresses. Should Lord and Lady David Ormont divorce, however, and Lord David remarries, while Lady David does not, his new wife would become Lady David, while his former wife would have no alternative but to place her forename before the 'Lady'—Margaret Lady David Ormont. She could not call herself Lady Margaret Ormont—unless she is Lady Margaret in her own right, as the daughter of a duke, marquess or earl.

Royal Warrants

Should a peer die and be succeeded by a relative other than his eldest son, the Sovereign may accord the new peer's brothers and sisters the titles and precedence which would have been theirs had their father been in possession of the peerage. Thus on his death in 1975 the 16th Duke of Norfolk was succeeded by a kinsman. The new 17th Duke's four sisters and three brothers were raised to the rank of a duke's daughters and younger sons by Royal Warrant.

Lords Spiritual

The Church of England

Ecclesiastics originally took part in the councils which were the precursors of the House of Lords in their capacity as administrators of large church estates and as government officials. The Bishop of Durham, for example, until the 19th century, was a prince-bishop, with extensive powers at least until the late 16th century in the English-Scottish border region. The reign of Henry VIII saw a change in the composition of the Lords in England. A clerical majority gave way to a lay one. In mid 1536 the composition of the House of Lords he summoned was 53 lay peers, 17 archbishops and bishops, 4 'keepers of spiritualities', 27 abbots, one prior and the Prior of St John of Jerusalem. In early 1539 it seems to have been 50 lay peers and 40 prelates and abbots.

Nowadays the two Archbishops of the Church of England (of Canterbury and of York) and certain of its bishops sit in the House of Lords by virtue of their office and are known as 'lords spiritual' as opposed to the 'lords temporal'. The Bishops of London, Durham and Winchester are entitled to sit in the House of Lords by virtue of their offices; there are also 21 other seats which are filled from among the remaining English diocesan bishops according to seniority of appointment to diocesan sees.

Precedence of Prelates

The Archbishop of Canterbury takes precedence in England and Wales next after Royal Princes, and the Archbishop of York next after the Lord High Chancellor, who follows the Archbishop of Canterbury. The Archbishops of Canterbury and York are metropolitans and thus have jurisdiction over the other diocesan bishops in their provinces: 30 and 14 respectively. An archbishop is addressed as 'Your Grace'. When one has resigned office, he is known by his surname, with, out of courtesy, his former title placed before it—'Archbishop Runcie'—although in fact he retains only his consecrated role as bishop. Nowadays he is granted a life peerage on retirement.

Bishops rank above barons and below viscounts. A bishop is addressed as 'My Lord'. Archdeacons, who superintend rural deans, rank next below bishops. Deans are heads of cathedral chapters; rural deans supervise the clergy within the archdeaconry.

Both Archbishops, together with the Bishop of London, are customarily created Privy Counsellors and are therefore accorded the style 'Right Honourable'. The wives of archbishops or bishops derive no rank from their husbands' appointments.

The formal prefixes are:

Archbishop	The Most Reverend and Right Honourable the Lord
Bishop of London	The Right Reverend and Right Honourable the Lord
Bishop	The Right Reverend
Archdeacon	The Venerable
Dean	The Very Reverend

Spiritual lords sign their forename followed by an indication of their diocese; for example, the Right Reverend David Sheppard, Bishop of Liverpool, signs himself 'David Liverpool'. In some instances the Latin form of the place-name, or an abbreviation of it, is used: thus, the signature of the Archbishop of Canterbury is 'George Cantuar'.

The Church of Scotland

The Church of Scotland is the national church in Scotland. The later Stuart kings imposed episcopacy on it, but in 1690 presbyterianism was finally established. There is therefore no hierarchy of clergy and all ministers are of equal status. The yearly General Assembly is the supreme authority. The Moderator of the General Assembly holds office for one year and presides over the Assembly. Although first among equals in the Church, he takes civil precedence in Scotland immediately after the Lord Chancellor of Great Britain. The formal prefix is 'The Right Reverend'.

The General Assembly is attended by ministers and elders—the eldership being a distinctive office to which men and women are ordained, to act along with ministers in church government and pastoral care. If the Sovereign is not present in person, he or she is represented by the Lord High Commissioner, who takes up residence in the Palace of Holyroodhouse in Edinburgh for the duration of the Assembly. The Lord High Commissioner and his wife are called 'Your Grace', even when they may be members of the royal family. The exception would be the Duke of Edinburgh, who would be referred to as 'Your Royal Highness', as he has precedence in Scotland over the Lord High Commissioner.

The Dean of the Chapel Royal in Scotland and the Dean of the Order of the Thistle are styled 'Very Reverend'. The appointments may be held by the same person. A former Moderator is entitled to the prefix 'Very Reverend'.

Baronetcies

The only inheritable honour bestowed apart from a peerage is a baronetcy. The Order of Baronets in England, said to be a revival of a more ancient Order, was instituted by James I in 1611, for gentlemen of good birth and with an estate of £1,000 a year. The condition was that they should, in three instalments, pay into the Exchequer a sum equivalent to three years' wages to 30 soldiers at 8 pence a day a man. The soldiers were needed for the settlement of Northern Ireland. The Baronetage of Ireland came into being in 1619 and that of Scotland (or of Nova Scotia)—to raise funds for the settlement of Nova Scotia and to hold land there—in 1625. After 1707 English and Scottish baronetcies ceased to be created, being replaced by baronetcies of Great Britain. Irish baronetcies, however, continued to be created until 1801, after which all newly created baronets were of the United Kingdom.

Among various privileges baronets of Nova Scotia were allowed to wear about their necks the badge of Nova Scotia, suspended from an orange tawny ribbon. In 1929 George V gave permission for all baronets, other than those of Scotland, to wear a badge (the arms of Ulster in the centre surmounted by a crown) suspended from an orange ribbon edged with dark blue.

Baronetcies are generally inheritable only by direct male heirs. There are special remainders, however, in some Scottish baronetcies. The present holder of the baronetcy of Dunbar of Hempriggs (cr. 1706), for example, is a baronetess—Dame Maureen Dunbar (or Lady Dunbar) of Hempriggs.

The premier baronet of England is Sir Nicholas Bacon (cr. 1611). The premier baronet of Scotland is the Duke of Roxburghe, by virtue of the baronetcy of Innes (cr. 1625). The premier baronet of Ireland is Sir Christopher Coote (cr. 1621). The premier baronet of Great Britain is Sir Francis Dashwood (cr. 1707).

Among the most famous and influential lines of baronets is that of Williams Wynn (cr. 1688), descended on one side from the medieval Welsh chieftain Cadrod Hardd (the Handsome), Lord of Talybolion, and on another from Welsh kings and princes, including Owen Gwynedd ap Griffith, prince of north Wales (d. 1169). With their seat at Wynnstay in Denbighshire, they came to own vast estates in north and central Wales, and in Shropshire. All the baronets since the third have been called Sir Watkin. This 3rd baronet, Sir Watkin Williams Wynn (1692–1749), who achieved wide political influence and was the most powerful (and popular) Tory in Wales (known as 'the Great Sir Watkin' and 'prince of Wales'), refused to consider a peerage, saying he was 'resolved to live and die Sir Watkin'. When he came to London to attend Parliament, 'Welshmen came out as far as Finchley and escorted him to town in a great procession'.[41] His elder son and successor, the 4th baronet, celebrated his coming of age in 1769

---

[41] While canvassing for a county election in 1720 he was escorted by 500 horsemen and wrote: 'To-morrow I roast a very large ox and hind, and intend to drink the town of Wrexham dry'. He was MP for Denbighshire 1716–41; for Montgomeryshire 1741–42; and for Denbighshire 1742–49. His election as mayor of Chester in 1736 prompted the *Gentleman's Magazine* to comment: 'the feasting continued several days, in so much that little business was done but by cooks and confectioners. Such appearance of gentlemen were never seen since Lord Delamere was mayor at the Revolution'. See Eveline Cruickshanks, *Political Untouchables* (London, 1979), pp. 19–20, 72.

by entertaining 15,000 people to an open-air dinner in his park when the bill of fare included 31 bullocks, 50 hogs, 50 calves, 80 sheep, 18,000 eggs, 150 gallons of milk and 60 quarts of cream.[42]

This Sir Watkin (1749–89), who married (as his first wife) Lady Henrietta Somerset, fifth daughter of the 4th Duke of Beaufort, was a cultivated man of his day. A friend of Sir Joshua Reynolds and David Garrick, he was also a generous contributor to the Welsh School in London. In 1776 he was a co-founder of the Concerts of Ancient Music and in 1784 one of the directors of the great Handel Commemoration in London. He retained the services of the blind John Parry (c 1710–1782) of Ruabon as resident harpist at Wynnstay.

Baronets are commoners, not peers, and are placed before knights in the order of precedence. A baronet is described by his forename (not necessarily the first) followed by his surname with the prefix 'Sir' (from Latin 'senior'—someone older or superior) and the suffix 'Baronet', usually abbreviated to 'Bt' or, less usually, 'Bart'. It is the practice to address a baronet as 'Sir' and then his forename without his family name, but incorrect to use the family name without his full forename, for example, 'Sir Walter' for 'Sir Walter Scott', but not 'Sir Scott' or even 'Sir W. Scott'.

A baronet's wife is, strictly speaking, 'Dame', the title once placed before her forename, but it has been the custom for many years to use 'Lady' placed before the surname—'Lady Scott'— not, on any occasion, 'Lady Emmeline Scott', unless she is the daughter of a duke, marquess or earl and thus holds a courtesy title in her own right (see p. 76). Should she be the daughter of

[42] Mark Bence-Jones and Hugh Montgomery-Massingberd, *The British Aristocracy* (London, 1979), p. 131.

a viscount or baron, she is 'the Hon. Lady Scott'. A baronet's widow is either called Dowager—'the Dowager Lady Scott'—or puts her forename before the title—Emmeline Lady Scott—to distinguish her from the wife of the successor to the title. If she remarries, or divorces and remarries, her position is the same as for peeresses (see p. 66).

At the end of 1995 there were some 1,300 baronetcies on the Official Roll of the Baronetage, kept at the Home Office.

Knighthoods and Orders

The honour of knighthood takes its form from the usages of medieval chivalry, from which also comes the method still normally used in Britain of conferring a knighthood by the touch of a sword (the 'accolade') by, or on behalf of, the Sovereign. ('Knight of the Carpet' was the term used for a man dubbed knight in time of peace.) The accolade has been used for ministers of religion, but not customarily when a clergyman of the Church of England is being appointed to an order of chivalry, for whom the use of a weapon of war is considered inappropriate.

By the end of 1995 there were approximately 3,100 Knights Grand Cross, Knights Commanders and Knights Bachelor, together with some 220 Dames Grand Cross and Dames Commanders. (The latter figure does not include peeresses who were also Dames, but includes those Dames who prefer to be known by another title, for example 'Lady', in respect of their husband's knighthood, or 'Mrs', or 'Lady' in respect of their birth as a daughter of a duke, marquess or earl.) In addition, some 82 peers held knighthoods (some more than one knighthood) and eight life peeresses and 11 peeresses (wives of peers) were also Dames.

Knights may be either Knights Bachelor or members of one of the orders of chivalry (see pp. 91–102), the newer of the latter being divided into classes. (There are also three Irish hereditary knighthoods.) They are all styled 'Sir' before their forename and surname. In former times their wives were styled 'Dame' before forename and surname. From the 17th century, however, it has been more the custom to style them 'Lady' before the surname:

'Sir Patrick and Lady Mayhew'.

If the wife of a knight has a courtesy title (see p. 76), she uses the appropriate prefix. If she has no courtesy title, it is incorrect to place her forename between 'Lady' and her surname (see p. 86).

Women appointed to the first (Dames Grand Cross) or second (Dames Commander) classes of orders are, however, styled 'Dame'—for example, Dame Janet Baker, DBE or Dame Iris Murdoch, DBE—but do not receive the accolade. (The wife of a knight in Scotland is still referred to as 'Dame' in deeds and other formal documents.[43])

Knights Bachelor carry no letters after their names, although the word 'Knight' may be added in legal or official documents. Knights and Dames of orders use initials denoting the order and the class to which they belong: for example, 'KG' for Knight Companion of the Order of the Garter; 'KBE' and 'DBE' for Knight Commander and Dame Commander respectively of the Order of the British Empire. These honours, dependent on grade, carry with them the right to wear, on appropriate occasions, various insignia—robes, badges, ribbons and other external distinguishing marks.

An ordained minister in the Church of England or in the Church of Scotland does not adopt the prefix 'Sir' if appointed a knight, nor does his wife become 'Lady'. But if appointed to an order, he uses the appropriate initials after his name. Roman Catholic clergy and nonconformist ministers labour under no such inhibition. They may receive the accolade (see p. 88) and adopt the prefix 'Sir'. Baronets in holy orders are styled 'Sir' and

[43] See, for example, the London *Daily Mail*, listing recent wills, of 6 June 1900, which refers to 'Dame Isabella Adair, widow of Sir Charles William Adair, KCB'.

persons who have been knighted may retain their style if they are subsequently ordained. A peer who is appointed a knight continues to style himself a peer. A knight who is created a peer continues to use any letters after his name (see p. 128).

Foreign nationals and citizens of Commonwealth countries of which the Queen is not head of State may be admitted to honorary membership of British orders, but do not style themselves 'Sir' or place letters after their name—though the decorations may be included as a courtesy in 'The London Diplomatic List' and they may wear the insignia—because they do not receive the accolade.[44] Permission from the head of State of the recipient's country is sought as a matter of courtesy before any such award is announced. The arrangements are made by the Foreign & Commonwealth Office. Recipients may wear the insignia on appropriate occasions, for example, at functions at the British embassy or high commission in their native capital or on formal occasions on visits to Britain.

The principal British orders are listed below in the relative positions assigned to them in the order of precedence, with brief notes about their origin, the degrees within them, and their robes and insignia.

[44] The Dutch conductor Bernard Haitink received an honorary KBE in 1977; Bob Geldof, of Irish nationality, was made an honorary KBE in 1986; the comedian Bob Hope, born in England but of US nationality, received his honorary CBE in 1976. Yehudi Menuhin was made honorary KBE in 1965. In 1985 he adopted British nationality and from then on was entitled to be called Sir Yehudi. He became OM in 1987 and a Life Peer (Lord Menuhin) in 1993.

Among foreign heads of State who have received honorary GCBs are President Ronald Reagan of the United States (1986), President Hosni Mubarak of Egypt (1991) and President Miguel de la Madrid of Mexico (1985).

The Most Noble Order of the Garter

Founded by Edward III, probably in 1348. The only rank is that of Knight Companion or Lady Companion. The Order consists of the Sovereign, the Duke of Edinburgh, the Prince of Wales, certain lineal descendants of George I, if chosen, and 25 Knights Companions[45] (excluding other sons of the Sovereign and Ladies of the Order). Queen Elizabeth The Queen Mother and the Princess Royal are Ladies of the Order. Foreigners, normally sovereigns, can be admitted as Extra Knights or Ladies. The Order is conferred on the personal decision of the Sovereign. Present members include several of the royal family, some foreign monarchs, a few distinguished peers, and a number of men and women who have achieved high office. Non-Scottish British Prime Ministers are offered the Garter, if they retire when in office. Among Knights of the Garter are Lord Callaghan, a former Prime Minister, Lord Carrington, a former Foreign Secretary, and Sir Edmund Hillary, mountaineer and conqueror of Everest. The late Lavinia Duchess of Norfolk (1916–95), widow of the 16th Duke, and former Lord-Lieutenant of West Sussex, was the first non-royal Lady Companion of the Order. Lady Thatcher, a former Prime Minister, was appointed Lady Companion in 1995. Among foreign monarchs who belong to the Order are the Grand Duke of Luxembourg, the King of Sweden and the King of Spain. The Queen of Denmark, the Queen of the Netherlands, and Princess Juliana of the Netherlands are Extra Ladies of the Order.[46]

[45] Statute of the Order (5 October 1954) provides for 25 Knights Companions. In practice there have been no more than 24 since 1963.

[46] Princess (former Queen) Juliana's mother, and Queen Beatrix's grandmother, Queen Wilhelmina (1880–1962; reigned 1890–1948), was the first queen regnant of a foreign state to receive the Garter, from George VI in 1944, in 'respectful admiration for the courage and steadfastness' she showed during the Second World War.

The reason for the choice of the Garter symbol and of the motto is the subject of attractive legend. According to one version, Edward III picked up the garter, accidentally dropped, of a court lady of whom he was enamoured. The King said to those who enjoyed the lady's embarrassment: 'Shame to him who thinks evil of it'. Some assert the lady was Katharine Grandison, wife of William de Montacute, 1st Earl of Salisbury; others that it was Joan, the 'Fair Maid of Kent', elder daughter of Edmund of Woodstock, Earl of Kent and youngest son of Edward I.

The Tudor chronicler Raphael Holinshed says that it was the garter of Edward's wife, Philippa of Hainault, which the King spotted and commanded a courtier to pick up. 'It is but some woman's garter', said the man. 'You, my masters', declared the King to the bystanders, 'do make small account of this blue garter, but, if God lend me life for a few months, I will make the proudest of you to reverence the like'.

Another version attributes the saying to the Queen—annoyed at the King's rebuke for allowing her garter to fall.

On ceremonial occasions Knights wear the Garter (dark blue velvet edged with gold and bearing the motto 'Honi soit qui mal y pense'—'Shame to him who thinks evil of it') on the left leg below the knee. The Mantle, of dark blue velvet, has a hood of crimson velvet. On the upper left of the Mantle, an embroidered Garter encircles the cross of St George. The Surcoat is of crimson velvet, lined with white taffeta. Fastened to the black velvet Hat (formerly by a band of diamonds) is a plume of white ostrich feathers. The gold Collar consists of 24 pieces—each a Garter surrounding the Tudor rose, connected by 24 knots of chased gold. Hanging from it is the George, an enamelled figure of St George on horseback slaying the dragon. The Lesser George, a gold badge, is worn from a blue ribbon over the left shoulder. In the centre of the Star is the cross of St George encircled by the Garter. On the death of a Companion, the heir delivers the Lesser George and Star to the Sovereign. The Collar, George and Garter are returned to the Central Chancery of the Orders of Knighthood.

Abbreviation: KG or LG.

Chapel of the Order: St George's Chapel, Windsor Castle.

The Most Ancient and Most Noble Order of the Thistle

Probably founded by James III (1460–88). Revived, with a statutory foundation, by James VII in 1687. It was revived again by Anne in 1703. The Order, conferred on the personal decision of the Sovereign, consists of the Sovereign and 16 Knights Brethren or Ladies. Royal Knights and Extra Knights may be appointed as the Sovereign decides. The late King Olav V of Norway was an Extra Knight. Queen Elizabeth The Queen Mother is a Lady of the Thistle. The Duke of Edinburgh and the Duke of Rothesay are Royal Knights. Among Knights are Lord Thomson of Monifieth and Viscount Whitelaw, former Cabinet ministers, the Earl of Airlie, Lord Chamberlain, and the late Sir Fitzroy Maclean of Dunconnel.

The Star, worn on the left breast, is a silver St Andrew's cross, rays placed between the cross's arms; in its centre is a green Thistle on gold, surrounded by a green circle, on which is the motto in gold letters: 'Nemo me impune lacessit' ('No one provokes me with impunity'). The Collar is of thistles and sprigs of rue in gold and enamel. From it hangs a gold and enamel badge of St Andrew holding his cross. The Mantle is of green velvet—on its left shoulder a representation of the Star. The Badge, when the Collar is not worn, is attached to a green ribbon passing over the left shoulder and resting on the right hip. It is of gold and contains the image of St Andrew holding his cross, with a thistle below his feet, and the motto 'Nemo me impune lacessit' around. The Hat is of black velvet with white plumes. On the death of a Knight, his heir delivers the Badge and Star to the Sovereign. The Collar and Badge are returned to the Central Chancery.

Abbreviation: KT.
Chapel of the Order: The Thistle Chapel, St Giles Cathedral, Edinburgh.

The Most Honourable Order of the Bath

Established as a separate Order by King George I in 1725, but with medieval origins. It is said that Sir Robert Walpole, Prime Minister and one of the original 37 appointees (who included the Dukes of Montagu, Richmond and Manchester), offered knighthood to a grandson and grandson-in-law of the 1st Duke of Marlborough. The offer was rejected by the Duke's formidable widow, Sarah (see p. 24). They would take 'nothing but the Garter', she said. 'Madam', Walpole replied, 'they who take the Bath will the sooner have the Garter'.

The Order takes its name from the symbolic bathing which in former times was often part of the preparation of a candidate for knighthood. It was enlarged in 1815 and again in 1847. It is awarded in recognition of conspicuous services to the Crown and is open to both sexes. The Great Master and First or Principal Knight Grand Cross is the Prince of Wales. There are two divisions, military and civil. Ranks in the Order, and their customary abbreviations, are:

Knight or Dame Grand Cross: GCB
Knight or Dame Commander: KCB or DCB
Companion: CB

The Mantle of a Knight and Dame Grand Cross is of crimson satin, with a Star embroidered on the left side. The Hat (not used since the reign of George V) was of black velvet, with a plume of white feathers. The gold and enamel Collar has 17 knots which link nine crowns and eight rose/thistle/shamrock emblems, giving a total of 34 pieces. Other insignia vary according to division. Thus the silver and gold Star of military Knights and Dames Grand Cross is in the shape of a Maltese cross against a star background. In the centre are three crowns surrounded by the motto of the Order: 'Tria juncta in uno' ('Three joined in one'). This circle is wreathed in two branches of laurel; beneath it on a scroll, the phrase 'Ich dien' ('I serve'). The Star of a civil Knight and Dame Grand Cross has no Maltese cross and the badge is in the centre of the Star. The Badge of the Order, worn by all ranks (by Knights and Dames Grand Cross hanging from a crimson riband passing from the right shoulder across to the left side), is a Maltese cross, in gold or silver-gilt for the civil division or gold (or silver-gilt) and enamel for the military division, bearing in the centre a rose, thistle and shamrock, issuing from a sceptre between three crowns.

Chapel of the Order: King Henry VII Chapel, Westminster Abbey.

The Order of Merit

Founded in 1902. The only rank is that of Member. It was originally restricted to the Army and Royal Navy, and to services towards the advancement of art, literature and science. Since the Statute of 1987 it has been open to: 'such persons, subjects of Our Crown, as may have rendered exceptionally meritorious service in Our Crown Services, or towards the advancement of the Arts, Learning, Literature and Science, or such other exceptional service as We see fit to recognise'. It is open to both sexes. Except for honorary members from overseas, the Order is limited to 24 people, appointed personally by the Sovereign. Dame Joan Sutherland, the opera singer, Lady Thatcher, Sir Michael Tippett, the composer, Air Commodore Sir Frank Whittle, the aviation pioneer, Professor Francis Crick, the scientist, and Sir Aaron Klug, President of the Royal Society, are among the members. Mother Teresa of Calcutta was made an honorary member in 1983. The Badge of the Order, suspended from a blue and crimson ribbon, is a cross of red and blue enamel surmounted by a crown. The words 'FOR MERIT', in gold letters on blue enamel, appear in the centre. The reverse contains the cypher of the reigning Sovereign. The badge of recipients who are members of the armed services is here distinguished through the addition, between the arms of the cross, of two silver and gilt crossed swords.

Abbreviation: OM.

The Most Distinguished Order of St Michael and St George

Founded in 1818 to reward citizens of Malta and the Ionian islands for services to the Crown. It has been much extended and modified since and today honours service overseas or in connection with foreign or Commonwealth affairs. The Grand Master is the Duke of Kent. Ranks in the Order, and their customary abbreviations, are:

Knight or Dame Grand Cross: GCMG

Knight or Dame Commander: KCMG or DCMG

Companion: CMG

The Mantle of Knights and Dames Grand Cross is of light blue satin, lined with scarlet silk. The Star is of seven rays of silver, with a small ray of gold between each. Superimposed is the cross of St George; in the centre of the Star is St Michael combating Satan, in a blue circle, around which, in gold letters, is the motto: 'Auspicium melioris aevi' ('Token of a better age'). The gold Collar of Knights Grand Cross consists of lions of England, Maltese crosses in white enamel, and the ornate cyphers SM and SG. The Chain of Dames Grand Cross is on a slightly smaller scale. The Badge, a medallion of St George and the Dragon on one side and a medallion of St Michael on the other, in a fourteen-point cross, is worn by Knights and Dames Grand Cross attached to the Collar or to a light blue ribbon with a centre scarlet stripe over the right shoulder.

Chapel of the Order: in St Paul's Cathedral.

The Royal Victorian Order

Instituted in 1896 by Queen Victoria, and in the Sovereign's personal gift, to reward services to the royal family, for example, by members of the Royal Household or the writer of a Sovereign's official biography. The Grand Master is Queen Elizabeth The Queen Mother. Ranks in the Order, which is open to both sexes, and the customary abbreviations, are:

Knight or Dame Grand Cross: GCVO
Knight or Dame Commander: KCVO or DCVO
Commander: CVO
Lieutenant: LVO
Member: MVO

The Mantle of a Knight or Dame Grand Cross is of dark blue satin edged with red satin. The gold Collar is composed of octagonal pieces (in their centres a gold rose with a jewel in the middle), and oblong perforated and ornamental frames. These frames contain parts of the inscription 'Victoria . . . Britt. Reg. . . . Def.Fid. . . . Ind. Imp.' (Victoria . . . Queen of Britain . . . Defender of the Faith . . . Empress of India) in white enamel. In the centre of the Collar is a gold medallion of Queen Victoria from which hangs the Cross. The Star of Knights and Dames Grand Cross is a silver chipped eight-pointed star, in its centre a likeness of the Badge, which is a Maltese cross with, in its oval centre, the Royal and Imperial cypher surrounded by the Order's motto 'VICTORIA'. This is worn hanging from a dark blue ribbon with a narrow edge either side of three stripes—red, white, red—from the right shoulder to the left side.

There are also three grades of the Royal Victorian Medal— Gold, Silver and Bronze.

Chapel of the Order: The Queen's Chapel of the Savoy in London.

The Royal Victorian Chain

Founded in 1902 by Edward VII, this is not part of the Royal Victorian Order. Besides Queen Elizabeth The Queen Mother, there are currently about 20 holders of the Chain, who include the Kings of Jordan, Thailand, Spain and Saudi Arabia. It is of different and lighter design than the Collar of the Royal Victorian Order.

The Most Excellent Order of the British Empire

Founded in 1917, chiefly to recognise service by civilians in the First World War, it is now the most widely conferred on civilians and service personnel for public services or other distinctions. The Grand Master is the Duke of Edinburgh. There are two divisions, military and civil. Ranks in the Order, which is open to both sexes, and the customary abbreviations, are:

Knight or Dame Grand Cross: GBE

Knight or Dame Commander: KBE or DBE

Commander: CBE

Officer: OBE

Member: MBE

The Collar for Knights and Dames Grand Cross is of silver gilt and incorporates six medallions of the royal arms and six of the Royal and Imperial cypher of George V. The chain linking them shows a crown and two sea lions. The Badge hanging from it shows the effigies of King George V and Queen Mary and the motto: 'For God and the Empire'. This may be worn by Knights and Dames Grand Cross from a rose pink riband passing from the right shoulder to the left side. The Mantle of Knights and Dames Grand Cross is of rose pink satin.

The Order includes a medal, the British Empire Medal (BEM), but since 1993 this has not been awarded in Britain.

Chapel of the Order: in St Paul's Cathedral.

Knights Bachelor

Although Knights Bachelor do not comprise an order of chivalry, knighthood is a dignity which has its origin in Britain in Saxon times. During the Middle Ages the use of the style 'Sir' prefixed to the Christian name of a knight became common usage. In the 17th century a Register of Knights Bachelor was instituted by James I, but this was discontinued. In 1908 a voluntary association now known as the Imperial Society of Knights Bachelor was formed with the encouragement of Edward VII and with the primary objects of continuing the various registers dating from 1257 and obtaining the uniform registration of every created knight. In 1926 the design for a breast badge to be worn by knights bachelor was officially approved and adopted: an oval medallion—an outer scroll enclosing a belted and sheathed sword and spurs. A neck badge is the official insignia for all knights bachelor appointed since the badge was approved on 30 November 1973.

Chapel of Knights Bachelor: the Priory Church of St Bartholomew in Smithfield.

Order of the Companions of Honour

Founded in 1917. The only rank is that of Member. It is awarded for service of conspicuous national importance and is open to both sexes. The Order is limited to 65 people (excluding honorary members). Mr Pierre Trudeau, former Prime Minister of Canada; Mr David Lange, former Prime Minister of New Zealand; Mr Anthony Powell, the author; Professor Stephen Hawking, the theoretical physicist; Sir John Gielgud, the actor; Dame Ninette de Valois, the former ballerina and ballet expert; and

Lords Healey and Tebbit, former Cabinet ministers, are Members. Mgr Derek Worlock, Archbishop of Liverpool (1920–96) was also a Member.

The Badge, suspended from a carmine ribbon and surmounted by a crown, is an oval enclosing a representation of an oak tree and a knight on horseback. Around the oval is the motto: 'IN ACTION FAITHFUL AND IN HONOUR CLEAR'.

Abbreviation: CH.

Imperial Service Order

Founded in 1902 to honour civil servants for their work throughout the British Empire. The only rank is that of Companion, which was discontinued in Britain after 1993.

The associated Imperial Service Medal is a long-service medal awarded on retirement.

Abbreviation: ISO.

The Most Venerable Order of St John of Jerusalem

Known as the Order of St John, incorporated by Royal Charter in 1888 and subsequent charters. The Order is the parent body of the St John Ophthalmic Hospital in East Jerusalem and the St John Ambulance, a body of unpaid volunteers which is active throughout the Commonwealth and in a number of countries outside it. It is not a State Order. Recommendations for membership are submitted by the Grand Prior (the Duke of Gloucester) to the Queen, who is Sovereign Head, and are made in recognition of services rendered to the charitable works of the Order. There are six grades. Membership does not confer any rank or title and members do not use the authorised letters after their names except in the context of their work for the Order.

Obsolescent Orders

There are some orders of knighthood in which no awards have been made for some years.

The *Order of St Patrick* was instituted by George III in 1783, partly to reward Irish peers (including the 2nd Duke of Leinster, the 5th Earl of Inchiquin, the 2nd Earl of Clanbrassil and the 1st Earl of Charlemont) for whom there were no vacancies in the Order of the Garter. In 1833 the maximum number of knights was fixed at 22. The last non-royal appointment to the Order was that of the 3rd Duke of Abercorn in 1922. Later, royal, appointments were the Prince of Wales in 1927, the Duke of Gloucester (Prince Henry) in 1934 and the Duke of York (Prince Albert, later George VI) in 1936.

The *Most Exalted Order of the Star of India* was instituted by Queen Victoria, with one class, in 1861. This first class of members consisted of ruling princes and chiefs, and British subjects considered to have deserved well. The order was extended to three classes in 1866. Its insignia were ornamented with many diamonds. No appointments were made after 1947.

The *Most Eminent Order of the Indian Empire* was founded by Queen Victoria in 1877. It was extended to two classes of members in 1886, and to three in 1887. The first class was occupied by those who merited reward for service to the Empire in India and by distinguished potentates of the sub-continent. No appointments were made after 1947.

The *Royal Order of Victoria and Albert*, for ladies, was instituted in 1862, but did not confer any rank on the recipient. Its last surviving holder, Princess Alice Countess of Athlone, daughter of Queen Victoria's youngest son (Prince Leopold, Duke of Albany), died in 1981.

The *Imperial Order of the Crown of India* was instituted in 1877 to commemorate Queen Victoria's assumption of the title Empress of India. It was 'to be enjoyed by the princesses of the Royal House who had attained the age of eighteen years and other female relatives of Indian princes and other selected persons'. The Queen, Queen Elizabeth The Queen Mother, Princess Margaret and Princess Alice Duchess of Gloucester are members. No appointments have been made since 1947.

Choosing Recipients of Honours, and Investitures

Reforms to the Honours System

In 1993 the Government reviewed and made changes to the honours system. The Prime Minister highlighted the following principles:

—awards are made on merit, for exceptional achievement or exceptional service;

—they are at different levels to reflect different levels of achievement;

—they are not automatic; and

—they emphasise voluntary service far more than before.

Except in the case of High Court judges, who continue to receive a knighthood on appointment (to reflect the independence of the judiciary), there is no longer an assumption that honours automatically attach to particular posts either in the public or in the private sector. Recommendations for honours do not now follow seniority in a job or appointment to it as a matter of course.

The British Empire Medal has been discontinued in Britain[47] and more MBEs are now appointed. The system of gallantry awards for the armed forces has been modified. They are

---

[47] The BEM continues for certain countries of which the Queen is head of State. The Honours List of 31 December 1994, for example, contained awards for New Zealand, the Cook Islands and Papua and New Guinea.

no longer linked to the rank of the recipient (see below).

Most honours are announced nowadays in one of the two annual sets of honours lists—one at the New Year and the other in June on the occasion of the Sovereign's official birthday. The Lists are published in supplements to the *London Gazette* and contain the names of those honoured and the honours conferred. The biggest number are contained within the Prime Minister's List and are at his or her recommendation. The Diplomatic Service and Overseas List is recommended by the Secretary of State for Foreign and Commonwealth Affairs, and the Defence Services List—covering serving members of the Armed Forces—by the Secretary of State for Defence. The prime ministers of those realms overseas of which the Queen is Sovereign, and who wish to use imperial honours, also make recommendations which are shown in further Lists.

Hereditary peerages are virtually never recommended. A typical Prime Minister's half-yearly List nowadays contains perhaps up to four life peerages, 40 knighthoods—most knights bachelor—125 CBs and CBEs, some 250 OBEs and about 650 MBEs (see pp. 95 and 99). Many more are nominated than are selected and numbers are carefully controlled to maintain standards.

An Honours Nomination form, obtainable from No. 10 Downing Street, enables any member of the public to put forward suitable candidates for honours. About a third of the awards in the Prime Minister's List have support from members of the public. Other candidates are nominated by government departments, covering the areas of public life for which they are responsible, and Lord-Lieutenants, who draw names from their counties.

The Prime Minister's List for each half year contains about 50 individuals recommended 'for political services' on the nomination of the leaders of those political parties wishing to make such recommendations. All political recommendations are shown to the Political Honours Scrutiny Committee, which has the duty of considering whether each individual is a fit and proper person to be recommended. The Political Honours Scrutiny Committee considers similarly all those recommended for life peerages in the half-yearly Lists and in the Lists of 'working peers' (see p. 46). The Committee consists of three senior Privy Counsellors, who are not currently members of the Government, and is appointed by Order in Council. All substantial payments to a political party by those recommended for life peerages or for political services must be declared to the Committee.

It is an offence, under the Honours (Prevention of Abuses) Act 1925, for anyone to offer to procure an honour for money or other valuable consideration, or for anyone to give money or take other action with the object of obtaining an honour (see Appendix 4).

Special Honours Lists are also issued on such occasions as a coronation or jubilee, on the dissolution of Parliament or on the retirement or resignation of a Prime Minister. Honours Lists do not contain the recipients of gallantry awards (see p. 109), except when a special List is issued to mark the successful conclusion of a military operation, such as the South Atlantic List in 1983 and the Gulf List in 1991. At other times Lists containing the recipients of gallantry awards are announced as occasion warrants.

Following the publication of an Honours List, investitures are held at which recipients of honours, other than life peers, receive the insignia of the honour. Knights receive the accolade. Knights and Dames, however, may adopt the prefix 'Sir' and 'Dame' from the date of the official announcement of conferral of the honour.

To enable the greater numbers receiving the MBE to attend a royal investiture, the Queen agreed to increase their frequency, both at Buckingham Palace and elsewhere, though she cannot conduct all investitures herself. The Queen has also made it possible for those gaining MBEs, OBEs or CBEs to receive their honour from their Lord-Lieutenant if they prefer.

New peers used to be invested by the Sovereign in special ceremonies. In 1514, for example, Henry VIII held a splendid one for the creation of Thomas Howard as Duke of Norfolk and Charles Brandon as Duke of Suffolk, and of Thomas Howard the younger as Earl of Surrey and Charles Somerset as Earl of Worcester.[48]

> They each made Garter king of arms a gift in recompense of the gowns they had worn before donning their new robes . . . . Suffolk's gown was magnificent and Garter wore it all day after the duke's creation. Estimated to be worth

---

[48] Newly created peers were normally escorted by peers of their new rank, but the only duke in 1514 (Buckingham, see p. 35) played no active part in the proceedings. 'For defaute of great astates', it was therefore recorded, 'the oon duke was created after toder'. Miller, *Henry VIII and the English Peerage*, p. 16. The 2nd Duke of Norfolk (1443–1524) had been commander of the victorious English forces at the battle of Flodden in 1513, despite the trouble one of his captains, Lord Dacre of the North, had had with the men of Bamburgh and Tynemouth: 'which at the furst shott of the Scottishe gonnys fledd from me and taryed noo lenger' (p. 143). His son Lord Surrey (1473–1554) succeeded him as 3rd duke. In 1515 Suffolk (d. 1545) was to marry the King's younger sister, Mary, Dowager Queen of France, whom the French called 'la reine blanche', and of whom a Flemish observer said, 'I think never man saw a more beautiful woman, nor one having such grace and sweetness'.

£200 and more, it was of violet velvet furred with sables, 'ramplisshed with scriptures of fyne gold inameled wheryn was wrytten *Loyalte me oblige*'.[49]

Such investitures ceased in 1615, during the reign of James I. A special ceremony, however, is held in the House of Lords when a new peer is introduced. He or she will be escorted by two peers of the same degree; his or her Letters Patent and Writ of Summons are presented to the Lord Chancellor; and he or she takes the oath of allegiance. On first attending the House of Lords a peer or peeress who has succeeded to a peerage will be greeted by the Lord Chancellor, but will not go through the same ceremonial as for a new creation.

---

[49] Suffolk got it back by giving Garter another one, of black velvet, £10 in angels and an annuity of £4. Miller, *Henry VIII and the English Peerage*, p. 16.

Decorations and Medals

The grant of peerages and baronetcies, the creation of knights and dames, and the admission of individuals to orders are not the only ways in which the Sovereign recognises merit. The conferment of a badge may in itself constitute an honour. This is the case with medals and decorations (that is, badges other than medals).

The list which follows below shows, in order of precedence, the principal decorations and medals awarded for distinguished or gallant services. It excludes campaign medals awarded by the Sovereign to participants in particular wars or campaigns; for example, the Defence Medal for defence service in the Forces or Civil Defence organisations in the Second World War; the 1939–45 Star awarded primarily to members of the Forces who served in that war; the Burma Star awarded to participants in the Burma Campaign; the Korea Medal awarded for service in the British Commonwealth forces on behalf of the United Nations in Korea; and the medal awarded to those who served in the Gulf War of 1991. Whereas most selective awards confer a right to append initials to the recipient's name, campaign medals do not (see also p. 115). The Territorial Decoration, instituted in 1908 for officers of the Territorial Army in recognition of long service, entitles the recipients to the initials 'TD' after their names.

Awards of decorations for distinguished services are normally published in the *London Gazette* in the periodic Honours Lists, but awards for gallantry are published at any time. Different awards are available for different categories of action; for example, some are made for members of a particular service only.

Certain medals and decorations confer not only distinction but also some financial benefit upon the holder. A tax-free annuity, raised in 1995 to £1,300 a year, is payable to both British and Gurkha holders of the Victoria Cross and of the George Cross.

The Victoria Cross (VC) was instituted in 1856 to honour outstanding valour in the presence of the enemy, and is the most highly esteemed of all British gallantry awards. Since it was inaugurated only some 1,350 awards have been made, nearly half being won during the First World War. The letters VC take precedence over any other a person has the right to append. It is normally won by servicemen, but may be conferred on civilians serving under military command.

The VC is worn on the left breast—a bronze cross with a crown surmounted by a lion in the centre, and beneath, the inscription 'FOR VALOUR'. It hangs from a crimson ribbon.

The first awards were announced in the *London Gazette* of 24 February 1857. On 26 June, in Hyde Park, Queen Victoria invested 62 of the 111 recipients from the Crimean war. A further 182 VCs were given for valour in the Indian mutiny of 1857–58.

The youngest recipients are Hospital Apprentice A. Fitzgibbon, of the Indian Medical Establishment, at the age of 15 years and 3 months in 1861, on the Anglo-French expedition to Peking; and Boy, 1st Class, J.T. Cornwell, RN, aged 16 years and 4 months, posthumously, at the battle of Jutland in 1916. The oldest seems to have been Captain W. Raynor, Bengal Veteran Establishment, at the age of about 69, in 1858.[50]

The George Cross (GC) was instituted in 1940 to honour great heroism or conspicuous courage. It was intended primarily for civilians, but is not limited to them. In practice more servicemen and women have received it than civilians. It has been bestowed not only on individuals but also on the island of Malta as a whole—for the island's gallant bearing under bombardment and blockade in the Second World War.[51]

The Conspicuous Gallantry Cross (CGC) was instituted in 1995 and is awarded to all ranks in the three armed services for conspicuous gallantry and great heroism. It replaces the DSO when awarded to officers for specific acts of gallantry, the CGM, the DCM and the CGM (Flying)—see below.

The Distinguished Service Order (DSO) was instituted in 1886 to honour gallantry and leadership in action displayed by officers of the armed forces of the Crown. The royal proclamation states:

> It is ordained that the order shall consist of the Sovereign, and of such members or companions as We, Our heirs or successors, shall appoint.

It could be awarded to officers of the Merchant Navy. A royal warrant of 1918 provided that the DSO should rank imme-

---

[50] There have been three cases of father and son receiving the VC and four cases of two brothers receiving it. No woman has yet won it. It is recorded that in September 1859 a gold representation of the decoration, without the inscription, was presented to Mrs Webber Harris, wife of the officer commanding the 104th Bengal Fusiliers, by officers of the regiment, for her 'indomitable pluck' in nursing those men of the regiment suffering in a cholera outbreak. Twenty-seven died in one night.

[51] There has been one case of one of two brothers being awarded the VC and the other the GC. In October 1995 there were 33 surviving holders of the VC and 47 (apart from that awarded to Malta) of the GC.

diately after the CBE. Since 1993 it has been open to all ranks and is now given in recognition of exceptional service in positions of substantial responsibility for command and leadership during active operations. It is the only gallantry award which cannot be given posthumously, as it is an Order and not a decoration.

The Royal Red Cross (RRC) was instituted in 1883 to recognise exceptional work by nurses rendered in any of the fighting services. There is also a second class of award known as 'Associate' (ARRC).

The Distinguished Service Cross (DSC) dates from 1914 (having been first instituted, as the Conspicuous Service Cross, in 1901) and was awarded to officers and warrant officers of the fighting services for distinguished conduct at sea in the presence of the enemy. It could also be awarded to officers of the Merchant Navy. Since 1993 it has been open to all ranks.

The Military Cross (MC) was instituted in 1914 and was awarded to ranks between major and warrant officer inclusive for gallant and distinguished services in the presence of the enemy on land. Since 1993 it has been awarded to all ranks.

The Distinguished Flying Cross (DFC) was instituted in 1918, for officers and warrant officers for bravery in air operations against the enemy. It could also be awarded to equivalent ranks of the Royal Navy and the Army for similar services. Since 1993 it has been open to all ranks.

The Air Force Cross (AFC) was instituted in 1918, for officers and warrant officers of the Royal Air Force for outstanding services in flying operations not against the enemy. It could also be awarded to equivalent ranks of the Royal Navy and the Army for similar services. Since 1993 it has been open to all ranks.

The Distinguished Conduct Medal (DCM) was instituted in 1854, for award to non-commissioned officers and men and women of the Army for gallantry and leadership in action. It has been replaced by the CGC.

The Conspicuous Gallantry Medal (CGM) was instituted in 1874, for petty officers and seamen and women of the Royal Navy, non-commissioned officers and men and women of the Royal Marines and equivalent ranks in the other armed forces, or for men of the Merchant Navy, for acts of conspicuous gallantry in the face of the enemy at sea. A similar medal, the Conspicuous Gallantry Medal (Flying; CGM), was instituted in 1942, for non-commissioned members of the armed forces for conspicuous gallantry in air operations against the enemy. Both have been replaced by the CGC.

The George Medal (GM) was instituted in 1940 and is awarded in circumstances similar to the George Cross where the act of bravery has not been sufficiently outstanding to merit the Cross. It can be awarded to foreigners.

The Queen's Police Medal for Distinguished Service (QPM), for regular officers of all ranks, was instituted in 1954.

The Queen's Fire Service Medal (QFSM) was instituted in 1954. It is awarded to members of recognised fire brigades for distinguished service and may also be awarded posthumously for gallantry.

The Distinguished Service Medal (DSM) was instituted in 1914, for petty officers and men of the Royal Navy and non-commissioned officers and men of the Royal Marines and equivalent ranks in the other armed forces, and for men of the Merchant

Navy for gallantry in the face of the enemy at sea which was not sufficient to merit the CGM.

The Military Medal (MM) was instituted in 1916, for non-commissioned members of the Army for bravery under fire. It has been replaced by the MC.

The Distinguished Flying Medal (DFM) was instituted in 1918, for non-commissioned ranks of the Royal Air Force for bravery in air operations against the enemy. It could also be awarded to equivalent ranks of the Royal Navy and the Army for similar services. It has been replaced by the DFC.

The Air Force Medal (AFM) was instituted in 1918, for non-commissioned ranks of the Royal Air Force for outstanding services in flying operations not against the enemy. It could also be awarded to equivalent ranks of the Royal Navy and the Army for similar services. It has been replaced by the AFC.

The Sea Gallantry Medal (SGM), formerly the Board of Trade Medal for Life Saving at Sea, is the only gallantry medal to have its origins in an Act of Parliament (in 1854). It can be awarded in silver or bronze. King Edward VII had a particular concern for it. In 1903–05 he agreed that it should be reduced in size (to 1¼ inches wide) to make it wearable on the left breast, and asked that recommendations should be submitted to him for approval. In 1909 he bestowed medals to recipients in person.

The Queen's Gallantry Medal (QGM) was instituted in 1974 to recognise acts of exemplary bravery. The medal is intended primarily for civilians but may be awarded to military personnel for actions for which purely military honours are not granted.

The British Empire Medal (BEM) was awarded for meritorious service, to men and women who did not qualify for the higher awards in the Order of the British Empire. It has been replaced in Britain by the MBE.

Commemorative Medals are issued by the Sovereign to selected recipients on such occasions as coronations and jubilees. A medal marked the Coronation in 1953 and a Silver Jubilee Medal was issued in 1977 to commemorate the 25th anniversary of the Queen's accession.

Medals no longer awarded include, for example, the Albert Medal (AM), first founded in 1866 to recognise 'heroic actions performed by mariners and others to prevent loss of life and save those in danger sustained by reason of shipwrecks and perils at sea'. It was reinstituted in 1867, with two classes—gold and bronze. Awards of the gold ceased in 1949. After that the bronze medal was given only posthumously. The Edward Medal (EM) was instituted in 1907 'for acts of gallantry in mines and quarries'—a 1st class of silver and 2nd of bronze. In 1949 awards of the silver ceased. In 1971 both medals were revoked and could be exchanged for the George Cross.

Awards of medals such as the Indian Distinguished Service Medal (1907–47) and Indian Order of Merit (IOM; military from 1837 and civil from 1902) ceased with Indian independence.

Some previous Campaign Medals include the naval medals that Elizabeth I authorised to commemorate the defeat of the Spanish Armada in July 1588. In 1643, early in the civil wars, Charles I instituted medals for those of his troops 'most forward in serving us'. They were of silver, 'containing our Royal image, and that of our dearest son, Prince Charles . . .':

And we do, therefore, most straitly command, that no sol-
dier at any time do sell, nor any of our subjects presume to
buy, or wear, any of those said Badges . . .'

Otherwise there would be 'pain and punishment as Our Council
of War shall think fit to inflict'.

Medals were distributed to commemorate Marlborough's
victories—Blenheim (1704), Ramillies (1706) and Malplaquet
(1709)—in the war of the Spanish succession. A medal was
instituted in 1746 to mark the defeat of Prince Charles Edward
(the Young Pretender) at the battle of Culloden, and was probably given by George II to his senior officers who fought in the
battle.

The Peninsular war (1808–14) and Crimean war (1854–56)
gave rise to various medals.

Arctic and Polar Medals have been, and still are, given to
commemorate explorations from 1818 onwards, and include
those of Scott (1910–13) and Shackleton (1914–16).

Certain Appointments Carrying the Right to a Prefix or Initials

There are also civilian appointments which carry the right to use a prefix or append initials in the same way as those relating to medals and decorations.

Privy Counsellor

In the days when the Sovereign ruled as well as reigned, the Privy Council was 'part of the court and, together with the Privy Chamber, formed its inner ring'. It was the inner advisory committee with executive powers. Today it exercises many functions of its own and also is the body by and with the advice of which the Sovereign exercises a large number of statutory and prerogative powers. All Cabinet ministers must be made members of the Council, and membership may also be conferred as a mark of honour on other persons of eminence in public affairs. Membership of the Privy Council gives a practical advantage to counsellors who are members of the House of Commons in that they are by tradition given priority when wishing to speak in the House.

Membership of the Privy Council (which is retained for life, except for very occasional removals) confers the right to be referred to and addressed in writing with the prefix 'The Rt Hon.' (for 'Right Honourable')—unless the person is entitled to a prefix of higher dignity such as 'Most Hon.'. The initials PC are sometimes used in books of reference for the sake of brevity to denote that a person is a Privy Counsellor, but it is incorrect to use these initials in any other circumstances after a person's name (except in the case of peers, who as such use 'The Right Hon.' or other prefixes of the kind [see p. 61]; without the initials PC it would not be apparent that they held this office). The letters PC, if used, follow all honours awarded by the Crown.

Queen's Counsel (QC)
In England a QC is a senior barrister, or solicitor holding the appropriate advocacy qualification, appointed on the nomination of the Lord Chancellor; in Scotland a QC is a senior member of the Faculty of Advocates appointed on the nomination of the Lord President of the Court of Session. QCs were originally appointed to represent the Crown in court cases. (During the reign of a king the expression used is King's Counsel—KC.)

Justice of the Peace (JP)
A local non-stipendary (that is, unpaid, lay) magistrate appointed by the Lord Chancellor on behalf of the Crown (in Scotland by the Secretary of State).

Deputy Lieutenant (DL)
A Lord-Lieutenant (the Sovereign's representative in his or her county) appoints a number of Deputy Lieutenants. A Deputy Lieutenant who, on retirement, has served for at least ten years may retain the style DL and wear the uniform on appropriate occasions. The letters DL should be placed after JP.

Member of Parliament (MP)

All Members of the House of Commons have the letters MP after their names.

Other Titles

Scottish Lairds and Chiefs

In Scotland the term 'feudal barons' is still used for the holders of the minor baronies of Scotland (with other freeholders). Until 1587 these barons sat in, and from 1587 elected commissioners to, the Scottish Parliament. Normally styled 'laird' they now have no special place in Parliament; they remain entitled to baronial insignia and add the name of their estate to their surnames. An example is the late Sir Nicholas Fairbairn of Fordell. They are to be distinguished from lairds who are not feudal barons but who are, or represent those who have been, considerable landed proprietors and add the name of their estate to their surname.

Similarly the Chiefs of Names and Clans in Scotland use legally a duplication of the patronymic or adopt the name of their ancestral seat as part of their names, as with MacLeod of MacLeod, Brodie of Brodie, Buchan of Auchmacoy, and Cameron of Lochiel; their wives are styled 'Madam' (for example, Madam MacDougall of MacDougall), though some now use the designation 'Mrs'. Like the eldest sons of lairds, their eldest sons and heirs may also use a duplication of their name, with the addition 'younger'. Instead of duplicating the patronymic, some Chiefs of Names add 'of that Ilk'; for example, the late Sir Iain Moncreiffe of that Ilk. A few Heads of Considerable Houses, who are not Chiefs of whole Names or Clans, employ the style 'Captain', such as the Captain of Clanranald (who is a MacDonald).

Irish Chieftains and Hereditary Knights

Irish titles are also used in Britain. Chieftains add the name of their ancestral seat, for example, The O'Donoghue of the Glens or The McGillycuddy of the Reeks. Other chieftains include The Fox, The O'Conor Don and The O'Donovan. The MacDermot of Coolavin is styled Prince of Coolavin but normally omits the latter title. Irish chieftains customarily use the prefix 'The'.

The three Irish hereditary knights must not be confused with baronets or members of the Orders of Chivalry. They are feudal dignities which date from the 13th century. They are: The Knight of Kerry (The Green Knight), The Knight of Glin (The Black Knight), and The White Knight, and are styled as such—for example, 'The Knight of Kerry'. Their wives, like those of Irish Chieftains, take the style 'Madam' before their surname, except for the wife of the Knight of Kerry, whose husband is also a baronet and who is therefore addressed as 'Lady'.

The Scottish Court of Session

Judges of the Court of Session, the highest Court in Scotland, are known as the 'Hon. Lord' or the 'Hon. Lady'—followed by their surname or a place name of their choice. Thus, the Hon. Lord Cullen or the Hon. Lord Marnoch. These titles, which are for life, are not part of the peerage system. The wife of a judge of the Court of Session is called 'Lady'—Lady Cullen or Lady Marnoch. The Lord President of the Court of Session, as the senior Scottish judge, may be awarded a life peerage, in which case he would become 'The Rt Hon. Lord'.

Esquires and Gentlemen

The abbreviation 'Esq.', written next after a man's name, is short for 'Esquire'. Legally it is a 'title, honour or dignity' pertaining hereditarily to the eldest sons and male successors of knights and younger sons of peers; also personally to military officers of and above the rank of Captain; Queen's Counsel; Royal Academicians; Justices of the Peace; and persons in positions of trust in the service of the Crown. To experts in rank and precedence it still legally denotes a position in the social scale; Queen Victoria created at least one esquire by Letters Patent, while in the commissions of army officers Captains and higher ranks are still described as 'Esquire', but junior officers are only described as 'Gentlemen'. However, because of the numbers involved, Esquire now tends to be used as a gesture of courtesy in ordinary correspondence. Except in the case of those indicated it is not essential to use 'Esq.'. (It is, however, incorrect to couple it with 'Mrs'; for example, John Smith, Esq., and Mrs Smith should be Mr and Mrs John Smith.)

'Gentleman' as a title is now seldom used, but pertains technically to all those in right of officially recorded armorial bearings. The officially certified possession of armorial bearings granted or confirmed by one or other of the Kings of Arms, is in fact legal evidence of the owners being 'Gentlemen of coat armour' and these 'gentry' are the equivalent of the *de* and *von* of the ordinary nobility of Europe. (In England a grant of arms has long been regarded as a form of recognition of social status, while in Scotland all arms are 'ensigns of nobility'.) The term 'gentleman' also pertains technically to certain professional persons and holders of higher degrees and offices, though personally and not hereditarily.

Academic and Professional Distinctions

Marks of distinction denoting academic and professional qualifications and status are not very widely used in everyday social life. For example, holders of university doctorates are not invariably addressed as 'Dr Jones', except in academic circles. (An important exception to this is the general medical practitioner who is habitually called 'Doctor' even though his or her medical degree may not actually be a doctorate. By tradition surgeons are addressed and referred to as 'Mr' or 'Mrs', whatever degrees they may hold.) Similarly, the use of initials after a person's name to indicate his or her university degrees or professional standing is, in general, restricted to academic or professional occasions. A guide to the meaning of the commonest initials in use for degrees of universities and membership of professional bodies is given below.

There are a number of professional or learned societies which have been formed to promote common interests and maintain standards, and have received royal charters. Membership confers distinctions which denote qualifications or status. There may be different levels of membership, and admission may depend on election (subject to qualifications) by current members, by passing an examination, or both. Admission by examination is most common for the lower levels of membership. A particularly coveted distinction in scientific circles is to be elected a Fellow of the Royal Society (FRS), the oldest scientific society in Great Britain, founded in 1660. A Fellowship of the British Academy (FBA), founded in 1901 to promote historical, philosophical and philological studies, is a comparable distinction in the field of general culture, as is membership of the Royal Academy of Arts (RA), founded in 1768, and of the Royal Scottish Academy (RSA), founded in 1826, among painters, sculptors and architects.

It is usual, though not essential, to use a special prefix when referring to a minister of religion. An ordained clergyman is called, for example, 'the Rev. John Smith'. (Rev. is an abbreviation for 'Reverend'.) This applies equally in the case of a woman. As with knights, the first name should be included; 'the Rev. Smith' is incorrect. A clergyman holding a doctorate may be called 'the Rev. Dr John Smith'. Deans and Provosts in the Church of England and former Moderators of the General Assembly of the Church of Scotland are formally referred to as 'the Very Rev.', bishops (and the Moderator of the General Assembly of the Church of Scotland) as 'the Rt Rev.' (Right Reverend) and archbishops as 'the Most Rev.'. An archdeacon is 'The Venerable' ('the Ven.').

Academic and Other Abbreviations

University and Comparable Awards

The nomenclature of degrees varies from university to university. Three grades are recognised. In ascending order they are Bachelor, Master and Doctor. A person who holds several degrees will normally write them in ascending order (in the order by which they are taken)—for example, William Brown, BA, PhD—although degrees from the universities of Oxford and

Cambridge are placed in descending order (in order of seniority)—for example, Arthur Black, PhD, BA.

The first degree at Oxford and Cambridge is called a BA (Bachelor of Arts) whether the course leading to it comprises 'arts' subjects (such as history or languages) or science subjects. In the four older Scottish universities (Aberdeen, Edinburgh, Glasgow and St Andrews) and in Dundee the MA (Master of Arts) is the first degree in the arts or social sciences faculties, although in other faculties the first degree is the appropriate Bachelor's degree. In all the other universities, courses of studies in the arts normally lead to the BA, as a first degree, and those in the sciences to the BSc (Bachelor of Science). This applies also to degrees of the Council of National Academic Awards, dissolved in 1993. (It awarded degrees and other academic qualifications to students who completed approved courses of study or research in establishments which did not have the power to award their own degrees.)

Other Bachelors' degrees include those given in: Architecture (BArch); Surgery (BCh, BS, ChB, or BChir); Civil Law (BCL); Commerce (BCom); Divinity, ie Theology (BD); Education (BEd); Engineering (BEng); Law (LLB); Letters (BLitt); Medicine (BM or MB); Music (BMus or MusBach); Philosophy (BPhil); Veterinary Medicine and Surgery (BVMS or BVSc).

Except for its special use in Scottish universities (see above), the degree of MA (Master of Arts) is a second degree, like other Masters' degrees. At most universities it implies further study, but at Oxford and Cambridge a BA may proceed to an MA without further study after the lapse of a minimum length of time and on payment of a fee, after which the person appends MA to his or her name and omits BA.

Other Masters' degrees are given in Surgery (MCh, MS, etc.), Dental Surgery (MChD or MDS), Librarianship (MLib), Letters (MLitt), Music (MMus), Science (MSc) and Humanities (MPhil). A doctorate is higher than a Master's degree, but possession of a Master's degree is not a prerequisite to registration for a doctorate. The PhD or DPhil (Doctor of Philosophy) is the most usual doctorate for postgraduate work of high quality. Despite the name, it is not limited to students of philosophy. Doctorates are also given more specifically in Divinity (DD), Dental Surgery (DDS), Medicine (DM or MD), and Science (DSc). 'Honorary' doctorates may also be conferred as a mark of esteem on distinguished persons a university wishes to honour. Honorary doctorates include LLD (Doctor of Laws), DLitt, DLit or LittD (Doctor of Literature) and MusD or MusDoc (Doctor of Music).

The letter D with another letter or letters after a name may refer to a 'diploma' awarded on successful completion of a course of study not leading to a degree; for example, some doctors add to their medical degrees DPH (Diploma in Public Health), DTMH (Diploma in Tropical Medicine and Hygiene) or DPM (Diploma in Psychological Medicine).

Membership of Chartered Bodies—Selected Examples
Institute of Chartered Secretaries and Administrators—has Associates (ACIS) and Fellows (FCIS).
Institute of Actuaries—has Associates (AIA) and Fellows (FIA).
Institute of Chartered Accountants in England and Wales—has Associates (ACA) and Fellows (FCA).
Institution of Civil Engineers—has Members (MICE) and Fellows (FICE).

Institution of Chemical Engineers—has Members (MIChemE) and Fellows (FIChemE).

Institute of Marine Engineers—has Members (MIMarE) and Fellows (FIMarE).

Royal Academy of Music—has Licentiates (LRAM), Associates (ARAM) and Fellows (FRAM).

Royal College of Organists—has Associates (ARCO) and Fellows (FRCO).

Royal College of Veterinary Surgeons—has Members (MRCVS) and Fellows (FRCVS).

Royal Institute of British Architects—has Members (RIBA). (It formerly had Fellows and Associates, and the letters FRIBA and ARIBA may still be used.)

Royal Society of Chemistry—has Graduates (GRSC), Licentiates (LRSC), Members (MRSC) and Fellows (FRSC).

Royal Society of Arts—has Fellows (FRSA).

The ascending order of levels of membership varies from body to body and no distinct rule can be given.

Other Qualifications

Certain solicitors in Scotland are members of one or other of two societies, the Society of Writers to Her Majesty's Signet (WS) and the Society of Solicitors in the Supreme Courts of Scotland (SSC).

The main nursing qualifications are Registered General Nurse (RGN) after a three-year training course, and Enrolled Nurse (EN) after a two-year training course. The qualifications RNMH, RMN, RSCN, RM and RHV denote specialisation in mental handicap, psychiatric or paediatric nursing, midwifery and health visiting respectively.

Order in Which Indications of Ranks and Honours Should be Placed

Some general rules and practices of particular importance on the relative positions in which custom or the order of precedence requires different indications of ranks and honours to be placed are listed below:

1   In general, indications of rank and status stand next to a person's name, either after any honorific terms of address before it, or before any initials that follow. Thus: 'the Rt Hon. the Lord Mackay of Clashfern' (not 'Lord the Rt Hon. Mackay of Clashfern') and 'Sir Nicholas Bonsor, Bt, MP (not 'Sir Nicholas Bonsor, MP, Bt').

2   Among the initials, the general rule is that the higher the honour indicated, the earlier its position. The special eminence of the VC and GC is marked by the fact that the initials VC precede all others to which a person may be entitled, and the initials GC precede all others except VC. After these two, the general rule is that initials relating to knighthoods and appointments in orders take first place, and those denoting medals and decorations (except VC and GC) follow. Thus Admiral of the Fleet the Lord Lewin, KG, GCB, LVO, DSC.

3   When a person holds appointments at different levels in different orders, the higher takes precedence over the lower. (A higher appointment in the same order subsumes the previous one.)

4   The initials QC or JP (QC precedes JP) follow those indicating membership of orders, and medals or decorations conferred by the Sovereign.

5   Initials indicating degrees and diplomas follow next. They are commonly placed in order of conferment (but see p. 125). Initials indicating membership of associations or societies follow those for degrees and diplomas, for example, Dame Mary Cartwright, DBE, ScD, DPhil, FRS.

6   The initials MP, which are conferred by custom and convention alone, come last. For example, a former Prime Minister, Sir Edward Heath, KG, MBE, MP.

7   Eminent persons who hold a number of honours are not generally described by all of them, but by the most distinguished ones. A Knight of the Garter might put only KG even if he had other orders, though there are exceptions to this custom. One set of initials never omitted from the name of someone entitled to them is that denoting a member of the House of Commons—MP.

Monarchs of Britain

English Kings and Queens

Royal Houses	Monarch	Dates of Reign
Norman	William I	1066–87
	m Matilda of Flanders	
	William II	1087–1100
	Henry I	1100–35
	m 1 Edith of Scotland	
	2 Adelaise of Louvain	
	Stephen	1135–54
	m Matilda of Boulogne	
Plantagenet	Henry II	1154–89
	m Eleanor of Aquitaine	
	Richard I	1189–99
	m Berengaria of Navarre	
	John	1199–1216
	m 1 Hadwisa of Gloucester	
	2 Isabella of Angoulême	
	Henry III	1216–72
	m Eleanor of Provence	
	Edward I	1272–1307
	m 1 Eleanor of Castile	
	2 Margaret of France	
	Edward II	1307–27
	m Isabella of France	

	Edward III	1327–77
	m Philippa of Hainault	
	Richard II	1377–99
	m 1 Anne of Bohemia	
	2 Isabella of France	
Lancaster	Henry IV	1399–1413
	m 1 Mary de Bohun (d. 1394)	
	2 Joan of Navarre	
	Henry V	1413–22
	m Catherine of France	
	Henry VI	1422–61
	m Margaret of Anjou	
York	Edward IV	1461–83
	m Elizabeth Wydeville	
	Edward V	1483
	Richard III	1483–85
	m Anne Neville	
Tudor	Henry VII	1485–1509
	m Elizabeth of York	
	Henry VIII	1509–47
	m 1 Catherine of Aragon	
	2 Anne Boleyn	
	3 Jane Seymour	
	4 Anne of Cleves	
	5 Katherine Howard	
	6 Katherine Parr, Lady Latimer	
	Edward VI	1547–53
	Mary I	1553–58
	m Philip II of Spain	
	Elizabeth I	1558–1603

British Kings and Queens

Stuart	James I	1603–25
	m Anne of Denmark	
	Charles I	1625–49
	m Henrietta Maria of France	
	Charles II	1660–85
	m Catherine of Braganza	
	James II	1685–88
	m 1 Anne Hyde (d. 1671)	
	2 Mary Beatrice of Modena	
	Mary II ⎫ (joint	1689–94
	William III ⎭ sovereigns)	1689–1702
	Anne	1702–14
	m George Prince of Denmark	
Hanover	George I	1714–27
	m Sophia Dorothea of Celle (div. 1694)	
	George II	1727–60
	m Caroline of Anspach	
	George III	1760–1820
	m Charlotte of Mecklenburg-Strelitz	
	George IV	1820–30
	m 1 Maria Fitzherbert (née Smythe)	
	2 Caroline of Brunswick	
	William IV	1830–37
	m Adelaide of Saxe-Meiningen	
	Victoria	1837–1901
	m Albert of Saxe-Coburg Gotha	
Saxe-Coburg and Gotha	Edward VII	1901–10
	m Alexandra of Denmark	

Windsor	George V	1910–36
	m Victoria Mary of Teck	
	Edward VIII	1936
	George VI	1936–52
	m Elizabeth Bowes-Lyon	
	Elizabeth II	1952–
	m Philip Mountbatten, Duke of Edinburgh	

Kings and Queens of Scots

Royal Houses	Monarch	Dates of Reign
MacAlpin	Malcolm II	1016–34
	Duncan I	1034–40
	m cousin of earl of Northumbria	
	Macbeth	1040–57
	m Gruoch	
	Lulach	1057–58
Canmore	Malcolm III	1058–93
	m 1 Ingibiorg	
	2 Margaret of England	
	Donald III Ban	1093–94
		1094–97
	Duncan II	1094
	m Octreda of Dunbar	
	Edgar	1097–1107
	Alexander I	1107–24
	m Sybil of England	
	David I	1124–53
	m Matilda of Huntingdon	
	Malcolm IV	1153–65

	William I	1165–1214
	m Ermengarde of Beaumont	
	Alexander II	1214–49
	m 1 Joan of England	
	2 Marie de Coucy	
	Alexander III	1249–86
	m 1 Margaret of England	
	2 Yolande of Dreux	
	Margaret	1286–90
Balliol	John	1292–96
	m Isabella de Warenne	
Bruce	Robert I	1306–29
	m 1 Isabella of Mar	
	2 Elizabeth de Burgh	
	David II	1329–71
	m 1 Joan of England	
	2 Margaret Drummond	
Stuart	Robert II	1371–90
	m 1 Elizabeth Mure	
	2 Euphemia of Ross (Countess of	
	Moray)	
	Robert III	1390–1406
	m Annabella Drummond	
	James I	1406–37
	m Joan Beaufort	
	James II	1437–60
	m Mary of Gueldres	
	James III	1460–88
	m Margaret of Denmark	
	James IV	1488–1513
	m Margaret Tudor	

James V   1513–42
m 1 Madeleine of France
   2 Marie de Guise
Mary   1542–67
m 1 Francis II of France
   2 Henry Stewart, Lord Darnley
   3 James Hepburn, Earl of Bothwell
James VI   1567–1625
m Anne of Denmark

Appendix 1

Husbands of Queens Regnant

Mary I married, as his second wife, Philip Prince of Spain, son and heir to the Holy Roman Emperor Charles V (who was also King Charles I of Spain). Before their marriage in 1554, the emperor elevated Philip to the kingship of Naples—to make it a marriage of equals. At the ceremony in Winchester Cathedral the titles of Philip and Mary were proclaimed: 'King and Queen of England, France, Naples, Jerusalem and Ireland. Defenders of the Faith. Princes of Spain and Sicily. Archdukes of Austria. Dukes of Milan, Burgundy and Brabant. Counts of Hapsburg, Flanders and Tyrol'. During his time in England, Philip was called King and expected by his wife to take part in affairs of Government. But he was never crowned. In 1556, on Charles's abdication, he and Mary became King and Queen of Spain. His kingship, and influence, in England ended with Mary's death.

Elizabeth I never married. Mary II (1689–94) reigned jointly with her husband King William III (1689–1702). The husband of Queen Anne, George Prince of Denmark (1653–1708), 'a simple normal man without envy or ambition . . . He had homely virtues and unfailing good humour', was created Duke of Cumberland in 1689. In 1702 Anne made him Generalissimo and Lord High Admiral. She also wanted to make him King Consort, but 'was tactfully prevented'. Prince Albert of Saxe-Coburg Gotha (1819–61), husband of Queen Victoria, was, uniquely, created Prince Consort in 1857.

On 24 April 1558 Mary Queen of Scots, resident at the French court since 1548, married the dauphin Francis, heir of Henry II of France. It was agreed that until he became king of France, Francis and Mary were to be known as king-dauphin and queen-dauphiness. He was granted the crown matrimonial of Scotland which conceded him equal powers with his wife.

In May 1565 Henry Stewart, Lord Darnley, Mary's second husband, was created Earl of Ross two months before his wedding. On 22 July he was created Duke of Albany. On 29 July, the day of their marriage, heralds proclaimed that Darnley (elder surviving son of the Earl of Lennox, or Master of Lennox as he would have been known in Scotland; or Prince Henry, as he was termed) should be called 'King of this our Kingdom', but he was not given the crown matrimonial.

On 12 May 1567 Mary's third husband, James Hepburn, Earl of Bothwell, was created Duke of Orkney and Lord of Shetland, Mary placing the ducal coronet on his head with her own hands.

Appendix 2

Titles Borne by Sons and Daughters of Sovereigns

The first Duke of Edinburgh was Prince Frederick Louis, grandson of George I, and future Prince of Wales (father of George III). Queen Victoria's second son, Prince Alfred, also bore the title.

The dukedom of York has traditionally (though not always) been given to the second son of the Sovereign since Edward IV granted it to his son Richard, one of the 'Princes in the Tower'. Henry VIII, Charles I and James II were all Dukes of York before becoming king—because of the death of an elder brother. The future George V and George VI were also Dukes of York before ascending the throne.

Gloucester has been a royal dukedom since Thomas of Woodstock, youngest (seventh) son of Edward III, was created Duke of Gloucester in 1385. Later dukes included the future Richard III and the youngest son of Charles I, Henry Duke of Gloucester (1640–60). Queen Anne's only surviving child, William (1689–1700), was known as Duke of Gloucester.

The first Duke of Clarence was Lionel of Antwerp, third son of Edward III. George Duke of Clarence (1449–78), brother of Edward IV and Richard III, was reputedly drowned in a butt of malmsey. William Duke of Clarence (1765–1837), third son of George III, became King William IV in 1830. The last Duke of

Clarence was Prince Albert Victor (1864–92), eldest son of Edward VII.

The dukedom of Kent has been in the royal family since 1799 when George III gave it to his fourth son, Prince Edward, who became the father of Queen Victoria.

No fewer than four (one source says five) of the infant sons of James II (then Duke of York), born between 1660 and 1677, were called Duke of Cambridge. None survived early childhood. A brother of this sad line was known as Duke of Kendal (1666–67). The dukedom of Cambridge was revived for Prince Adolphus, seventh son of George III, in 1801. It died out with the death of his son, George William, in 1904.

Other royal dukedoms include Albany, an ancient Scottish title, last borne by the son of Queen Victoria's youngest son, Prince Leopold, Duke of Albany. In 1644 Charles I created the dukedom of Cumberland for his nephew Prince Rupert of the Rhine (1619–82), third son of his sister Elizabeth, Queen of Bohemia. Cumberland was also inherited by the descendants of George III's fifth son, Prince Ernest. The dukedoms of Albany and Cumberland have been suspended since the First World War. Sussex was borne by the sixth son of George III, Prince Augustus, and Connaught by the third son of Queen Victoria, Prince Arthur, and died out with the death of his son in 1943.

Although treated with the honour considered their due, daughters of sovereigns were not necessarily called 'Princess'. The daughters of Henry VIII were known as 'Lady Mary' and 'Lady Elizabeth' ('My Lady Elizabeth's Grace') before becoming queen. Mary also signed herself 'Daughter of England'. Even the future queens Mary II and Anne could be known before their marriages as 'Lady Mary' and 'Lady Anne'. The title princess does not appear to have been used on a regular, everyday basis until the 18th century.

The daughters of a Scots sovereign were proclaimed 'Dochtour of Scotland' by the Lord Lyon King of Arms at their baptism.

Appendix 3

The 'Bedchamber Plot'

In May 1839 the Government of the Whig Prime Minister, Lord Melbourne, to Queen Victoria's dismay, resigned over the question of suspending the constitution of Jamaica. The Tory leader, Sir Robert Peel, was invited to form a Government, but made it known that he expected to make changes in the higher offices of the Court and among the Queen's Ladies, nearly all of whom were related to members of, or supported, Melbourne's Cabinet. Melbourne 'put it into the Queen's head' to retain her 'non-political' Household intact, as he did not want a 'contingent of Tory ladies let loose in the Palace'.

> 'I said', wrote the Queen about her audience with Peel, 'I could *not* give up *any* of my Ladies, and never had imagined such a thing. He asked if I meant to retain *all*. "*All*", I said. "The Mistress of the Robes and the Ladies of the Bedchamber ?" I replied, "*All*"—'.

Peel explained that these Ladies were married to opponents of his projected Government. They would, the Queen contended, not interfere in politics, for she never talked politics with her Ladies.[52]

---

[52] See Elizabeth Longford, *Victoria RI* (London, 1964), pp. 109–13.

Peel gave up his attempt to form a Government and Melbourne resumed office. There would be no more conflict on this issue, however. When Melbourne finally resigned in 1841, Peel successfully formed a Government. In future the Queen had to change only her Mistress of the Robes.

In 1886 Gladstone failed 'to enlist a complete royal Household'. The post of Mistress of the Robes remained unfilled for a time because 'no Liberal duchess would accept'.

Appendix 4

Sale of Honours

In contrast to his Tudor predecessors, James I created many peers and is said to have doubled the numbers of the English peerage during his reign (1603–25). He began to sell peerages—baronies at £10,000 each, for example—and baronetcies to raise money. He was exceedingly generous with knighthoods and was known to have commanded 500 men to come to London to receive the accolade in one ceremony. It was not unknown for a man who refused knighthood to be fined. James's favourite George Villiers, Duke of Buckingham, was accused of trafficking in honours. When the House of Commons took steps to impeach the Duke in 1628, Lord Robartes, a Cornish tin magnate, gave evidence that Buckingham had forced him to purchase a barony 'at the price of £10,000'—'an involuntary venal peer', as he has been called. The practice of selling honours continued after James's death, for his 17th-century successors, often at odds with Parliament, found it very difficult to raise funds without the approval of the House of Commons.

In the late 19th century and into the 20th century, honours were from time to time sold by the government in power in efforts to raise funds for party political purposes, or bestowed for questionable political reasons. The practice caused indignation and disquiet, not least to George V. During the premiership of David Lloyd George (1916–22) the sale of honours was arranged by middlemen. A speech in the House of Lords in 1922 testified to the magnitude of the scandal:

> The Prime Minister's party, absolutely penniless four years ago, has . . . amassed an enormous parliamentary chest, variously estimated at between one and two million pounds. The strange thing about it is that it has been acquired during a period when there has been more wholesale distribution of honours than ever before, when less care has been taken with regard to the service and character of recipients than ever before.

It has been said that the price of a peerage ranged between £50,000 and £100,000; of a baronetcy between £20,000 and £40,000; and a knighthood cost about £20,000. In 1925 the Honours (Prevention of Abuses) Act, aimed at stopping the improper bestowal of honours, came into force. In 1933 Maundy Gregory, most notorious of the honours traffickers, was sentenced to two months' imprisonment and a fine of £50—after a trial kept short to avoid further scandal.

Addresses

Cabinet Office, Great George Street, London SW1P 3AL.

Central Chancery of the Orders of Knighthood, St James's Palace, London SW1A 1BH.

College of Arms, Queen Victoria Street, London EC4V 4BT.

Court of the Lord Lyon, HM New Register House, Edinburgh EH1 3YT.

Home Office, Constitutional Unit, 50 Queen Anne's Gate, London SW1H 9AT.

House of Lords, London SW1A 0PW.

Imperial Society of Knights Bachelor, 21 Old Buildings, Lincoln's Inn, London WC2A 3UJ.

The Scottish Office, Home Department, St Andrew's House, Edinburgh EH1 3DE.

Further Reading

The Complete Peerage. 6 volumes (paperback; reprint of the work, by George Edward Cokayne, first published in the late 19th century).
ISBN 0 86299 442 X   Alan Sutton Publishing   1988

The Scots Peerage.   Douglas   1904–14

British Gallantry Awards.
Abbott, Peter Edward and Tamplin, John Michael.
2nd edition.   Nimrod and Dix   1971

Clans, Septs and Regiments of the Scottish Highlands.
Adam, Frank.
8th revised edition.
ISBN 0 7179 4500 6.   Clan Books, Stirling   1970

The Royal Encyclopedia.
Allison, Ronald and Riddell, Sarah (editors).
ISBN 0 333 53810 2.   Macmillan Press   1991

The British Honours System.
Bedells, J.H.B.
ISBN 0 904858 00 6   The Heraldry Society   1974

The Queen's Orders of Chivalry.
De La Bere, Brigadier Sir Ivan.   Spring Books   1964

Royal Ceremonies of State.
Brooke-Little, John.
ISBN 0 600 37628 1   Country Life Books   1980

Burke's Dormant and Extinct Peerages.
New impression of the 1883 edition.
ISBN 0 85011 003 3   Burke's Peerage   1969

Burke's Guide to the Royal Family.
ISBN 0 85011 015 7.   Burke's Peerage   1973

Burke's Peerage and Baronetage. 105th edition.
ISBN 0 85011 034 3   Burke's Peerage   1980

*Debrett's Correct Form: Standard Modes of Address for
Everyone from Peers to Presidents.* Revised edition.
ISBN 0 7472 0658 9. (Hardcover)   1992
ISBN 0 7472 3926 6. (Paperback)   Headline   1992

*Debrett's Peerage and Baronetage, with Her Majesty's
Royal Warrant Holders.*
ISBN 0 333 41776 3.   Macmillan   1995

People of Today.
ISBN 1 870520 24 6.   Debrett's   1995

The Honours System: Who gets What and Why.
De-La-Noy, Michael.
ISBN 1 85227 339 9.   Virgin Books   1991

Ribbons and Medals.
Dorling, H.
ISBN 0 540 07120 X.   G. Philip   1974

British Battles and Medals. 4th edition
Gordon, Lawrence Lee.
revised by Edward C. Joslin.   Spink & Son   1971

Henry VIII and the English Peerage.
Miller, Helen.
ISBN 0 631 13836 6   Basil Blackwell   1986

The Monarchy (Aspects of Britain series).
ISBN 0 11 701633 0   HMSO   1991

Peerage Law in England.
Palmer, Francis Beaufort.   Stevens and Sons   1907

A History of the Coronation.
Passingham, W.J.   Sampson Low   1937

New Extinct Peerage, 1884–1971. (Extinct,
Abeyant, Dormant and Suspended Peerages
with Genealogies and Arms.).
Pine, Leslie Gilbert.
ISBN 0 900455 23 3   Heraldry Today   1972

The Knights of England. 2 volumes.
Shaw, William A.
ISBN 0 900455 11 X.   Heraldry Today   1971

*The English Court: from the Wars
of the Roses to the Civil War.*
Starkey, David, and others.
ISBN 0 582 49281 5.   Longman   1987
(Paperback)

*Titles and Forms of Address: a Guide
to their Correct Use.* 19th edition.
ISBN 0 7136 3132 5.   A. & C. Black   1990

Vacher's Parliamentary Companion.   Published quarterly.

*The Queen has been Pleased:
The British Honours System at Work.*
Walker, John.
ISBN 0 436 56111 5.   Secker & Warburg   1986

Who's Who. A. & C. Black.   Published annually.

Index

Printed in the United Kingdom for HMSO
Dd. 301671 C30 8/96 571 CCN 9385 4185